MW01274009

RETURN

—— *to the* ——

Father's Heart

So the Earth Will Survive
(Malachi 4:6)

ROBERT B. SCOTT

WESTBOW®
PRESS
A DIVISION OF THOMAS NELSON
& ZONDERVAN

Scripture quotations taken from the New American Standard Bible®, Copyright © 1960, 1962, 1963, 1968, 1971, 1972, 1973, 1975, 1977, 1995 by The Lockman Foundation. Used by permission. (www.Lockman.org)

WestBow Press books may be ordered through booksellers or by contacting:

WestBow Press
A Division of Thomas Nelson & Zondervan
1663 Liberty Drive
Bloomington, IN 47403
www.westbowpress.com
1 (866) 928-1240

ISBN: 978-1-4908-8879-8 (sc)
ISBN: 978-1-4908-8880-4 (hc)
ISBN: 978-1-4908-8878-1 (e)

Library of Congress Control Number: 2015910543

Print information available on the last page.

WestBow Press rev. date: 07/14/2015

Contents

Introduction

The most important activity on earth today is the turning of the hearts of God's children to their Father God, and the turning of parents' hearts to their children and the children's hearts to their parents (Mal. 4:6). Otherwise, all life on this earth will perish.

One way or another, Jesus is coming back. But He needs a people prepared to be His bride, a people who have sought and received the grace of forgiveness to forgive their fathers and turn their hearts to their Father Love.

This is the story of how this verse is beginning to be fulfilled. It is the story of how Christians who have struggled with the drama of soap opera lives are finding freedom in Jesus and in the Father's spirit of forgiveness.

It is also a story of how each Bible verse has more than one meaning. This Elijah to come will teach the value of children. Jesus the Restorer will direct this man and/or ministry to bring the hearts of the fathers back to their children and the hearts of the children back to their fathers. The hearts of God's children will also turn back to the heart of Father God. "Elijah" will awaken the hearts to love.

Father God will reclaim His children, as will biological fathers. Pastoral fathers will repent and begin to teach and reclaim Jesus and Father Love. Governmental leaders who repent will call their nations back to Jesus and our Father.

The many throwaway children of today's society will be brought back into the fold of the family. At the same time, however, the effects of child abuse will also be felt. Brother will betray brother, the father his child, "and children will rise up against parents and cause them to be put to death" (Mat. 10:21). Some will turn to love, and some won't. When a child is unforgiving to his parents, he can want to kill them.

Our Freedom Blog on both of our sites exploded with questions from people who have been trapped in unforgiveness and in problems that would have been unheard of fifty years ago. The challenge of bringing the hearts of the children to their fathers by forgiving them and of turning their hearts to their Father God is greater than ever, and it is more crucial than ever.

We were obliged to paraphrase the blog comments and refuse to publish any names, so we lose the power of direct quotes and the personal effect of the names. Such are the limits of publication. We thank God that you will still feel the impact of these powerful testimonies.

A storm of soap opera style comments and questions ensued when a man who gave a false name showed the symptoms of a son who had not forgiven his father. Some bloggers named the syndrome this man was afflicted with by his name. Much polemic followed, until a prayer warrior prayed all night for clarity on the situation. This is a quote we couldn't paraphrase since we know it came directly from God and this woman of God would not be offended at having her words published. God inspired several prayers that we post and reprint here.

This blogger spent a whole night reading and praying over this … syndrome and all those that have become the victims of it. She relates, "I choose to declare to all [those with this syndrome] and others that your sins are forgiven. We forgive you for your anger rage, your betrayals, your hurting words, your lies, your tantrums, your cursing, your petty thefts, your debts, your sabotages, your inconsideration, your abuses, your undermining, your jealousies, your need to brag and compete, your perversions, your lust, your cruelties, your selfishness, your denials, your insanities, your infatuation with your body, your degrading, your inversions, your contemptuous belittlements, your poutiness, your sympathy seeking, your vengefulness, your disputing, your rebellion to the truth, your vows of hatred, your errors of judgment, your role playing, your condemnations, your false respect, your unthankfulness, your ingratitude, your incompetence, and most of all we forgive you for locking out spiritual growth in your life because of your inability to forgive others or yourself. You are released into a new day, a fresh start, and into the grace of forgiveness."

"To those enslaved by [this] syndrome we pray an infilling of your heart with an understanding of what it is to be loved, with a strength to turn over to Jesus all the things that have held you back, with the ability to seek peace and be a peacemaker, the strength to ask for forgiveness when or if you fall back into the old ways, the humility to be teachable, the desire to bless others and not curse them, the grace to be thankful and grateful, and the understanding of how to encourage your heart and your families with the Word of God. We bless you with vision and purpose so that you will grow to be the man that God has meant you to be. This we pray in Jesus name, amen."

"We pray for the friends and families of those who live with [this] syndrome. We bless you with the grace of forgiveness, the strength to give a fresh start, the wisdom to call for the favor of God into all relationships in dealing with those who have been struck down into this syndrome, the wisdom to speak God's words into their soul, and the grace to love the unlovable in such a way that it encourages change and growth in their life and yours. We pray for healing in your family, your relationships, and your walk with Jesus and we thank our Father for your protection and the protection of your boundaries. In Jesus' name we bless you. Amen."

"To all those who have been hurt by this … syndrome, we pray that the grace of forgiveness will reside in your soul, that with each new day you will thank Jesus for dealing with the person stuck in this syndrome, and that in this new day you will learn more about getting free in Jesus. We pray that with each new day you will turn over your pain, and anything that would tempt you to move or stay in unforgiveness. We pray for your peace and for the healing of your soul so that you may walk as the light of God and as the sons of God. May your joy in Jesus never fail. In Jesus' name we pray, amen."

"For all those stuck in this … unforgiveness and for those that have been hurt by it, we pray peace into your souls so that you can turn over to Jesus all roots of bitterness that seek to corrupt and destroy your life. Walk strong, hand in hand with Jesus. In Jesus' name, amen."

Shortly after this prayer was posted, we received this comment from a blogger, saying he had told his sister to read this believer'sprayers. She did, and then she tried it on her brother-in-law, a father-hater who resisted and justified himself until as she identified every game he played and kept forgiving him, he broke down and cried. He asked for forgiveness, calling out to Jesus to forgive him and give him the empowerment to forgive his father and asked for the healing of his soul.

A few minutes later this comment came in from another blogger saying that he too was attacked with this syndrome. He felt that his life was a wreck because of the hatred that he had for his dad because of what his dad had said and done to him. It took two hundred and four pages to enumerate his certainty that he had the right to never forgive his dad, ever! He then decided to write out a list of all the things that he hated about himself and his life and after seventy-one pages, he understood that he himself exhibited the unforgiving stance that was making him exactly like his dad whom he hated. He kept thanking Father Love for His grace for the spirit of forgiveness to be manifest in his life, but to no avail. Then he read the prayers. He then put his name on the list of things he hated about his life as he realized he needed to forgive himself. He declared to his heavenly Father that he forgave himself. He then put his dad's name on the two-hundred-and-four page list. He then declared that he forgave his father for every offense, every hurt, and every item he had on that list. When he finished the list he laid down drained physically and mentally. He got a phone call about fifteen minutes later; it was his dad calling. It was the first time he had spoken to him in nearly ten years. He heard his father ask him to forgive him for all the pain and hurt that he had caused him. Vince told his father, spoke it out right there and then in his ear that yes, he forgave him. When his father asked him to go out to dinner with him, he accepted with joy. He felt God's mercy and goodness; words could not convey his thankfulness to his Father in heaven for this joyful breakthrough in his life. He thanked the woman of God for her perseverance in this written prayer that set him free.

This comment by another blogger followed with him saying that he had been putting up walls refusing to see the truth about the state of his life. It took some time but finally he realized that this same syndrome attacked him. He had vowed to never forgive his father. He knew that he was plagued with sudden calamities and hardships. Jobs were an issue, ever changing and never satisfying. He found it very difficult to even think that he could possibly be the problem. But he knew it was not his dad's fault but his own that had caused the state of failure and disorder in his life. After reading the first testimony, he knew the truth; he needed Jesus and the grace to forgive himself and all those in his life that he had seen as responsible for the chaos in his life. Then he read the prayers, and he was transfixed, weeping, his soul and the longing of his heart laid bare to Jesus.

We believe this is part of a small beginning of forgiveness and reconciliation between sons and fathers. We believe this book will be a part of turning the hearts of God's children to their Father, whose name is Love (1 John 4:8). As with our blog, we believe many who are not yet God's children will also be drawn to Jesus by the Father so He can reveal the Father to them. God wants to prepare them to be part of the Bride of Jesus, the end-time church that will be prepared to establish a marriage covenant with Him, to be spared from the Great Tribulation and to stand before the Son of Man (Luke 21:36).

While a specific "Elijah" is prophesied to emerge, a number of ministries are endeavoring, in the spirit of Elijah, to fulfill two important end-time Bible prophecies. Malachi 4:6 says, "Behold, I am going to send you Elijah the prophet before the coming of the great and terrible day of the [Eternal]. He will restore the hearts of the fathers to their children and the hearts of the children to their fathers, so that I will not come and smite the land [the earth] with a curse."

John the Baptist came before Jesus' first coming to prepare the way before Him: "And he will turn many of the sons of Israel [the believers] back to the [Divine Master] their God. It is he who will go before Him in the spirit and power of Elijah, TO TURN THE HEARTS OF THE FATHERS BACK TO THE CHILDREN, and the disobedient to the attitude of the righteous, so as to make ready a people prepared for the [Divine Master]" (Luke 1:16-17).

Notice that the verse before Malachi 4:6 speaks of an end-time disobedience. It calls us to remember something some TV evangelists are now saying is done away and nailed to the cross, the law: "Remember the law of Moses My servant, even the statutes and ordinances which I commanded him in Horeb for all Israel [the word also means the believers]."

In other words, all believers today aren't called to the "grace revolution," which is a lawless rebellion, but to remembering all 613 laws of Jesus, who is the "My" mentioned here in the First Testament, which Jesus doesn't consider "old' and the 613 that He added later in the New Testament, since this is an end-time prophecy.

Jesus said this work of Elijah "will restore all things…" (Mat. 17:11). He will restore truths from the Bible that have been lost to Christians today, truths that will set them free (John 8:32). He will restore all those many laws that preachers think is legalism.

We pray that those who have eyes to see and ears to hear will prove these truths from God's Word and hold fast to them in these last days (1 Thes. 5:21). The Father may be turning you, or turning you back, to His heart, a heart of love. We pray God's hundredfold blessings of *shelam* and *shalom* and His spirit of forgiveness and repentance upon our readers.

CHAPTER 1

Soap Opera Lives Washed Clean by Jesus

Years ago a popular comedienne produced a funny spoof on a familiar soap opera she called, "As the Stomach Turns." The topsy-turvy lives of soap opera characters can indeed turn your stomach. The problems you see are gut wrenching.

What is especially disheartening is that Satan has turned so many Christian lives and families into heartbreaking soap operas. God foreknew these attacks on His people in the last days, and He provided a solution, if we are willing to implement it.

Soap operas got their name from the soap companies that originally sponsored them. The term seems quite appropriate since soap opera lives need lots of cleaning up. The unholy dramas many believers experience need the blood of Jesus for the cleansing. The root causes also need to be discovered.

What has caused the hearts of children to be turned away from their parents, especially their fathers, in this end time? Why have families broken up? Why do God's children today see *their* Father as distant or even cruel? Why have their hearts not turned to Him in love and trust so they could be a people prepared for their Bridegroom Jesus? Why are believers mocking God and turning off nonbelievers by the dramas and even scandals of their hypocritical lives? Why haven't they known the emotional and even physical healing their Father has promised them?

Many of the visitors to our Freedom Blog are discovering the answers to those questions. In this book we will endeavor to bring answers, some of which have been partially presented in our previous books, available on the bookstore tab at www.freedomchurchofgod.com.

Our Father wants His people free, and we believe we are some of the ones who are called to be instruments of that freedom in these last days. The testimonies you have read and will read in this book confirm that this process of freedom has begun. Freeing truths that have been lost for centuries to the Christian world are being restored. Miracles are occurring. Lives are changing. Long-term hurts and pains are being healed.

Lives Changed, People Set Free

As our heads were swimming recently with the steady stream of praise reports that were filling our hearts with joy, a pastor who has followed the blog faithfully and seen great changes in himself and his congregation wrote and said that he thought that the blog should have as its title, "Praise Jesus! The site of miracles!" He went on to say that he was passing on the miraculous results of prayer to other pastors.

A man who had sustained a severe bite on his hand received revelation from others on site and he shared that he had gone to bed the night before, thanking his Heavenly Father for His spirit of forgiveness. Also, he thanked Him that by the stripes of Jesus his hand was healed. When he awake the next morning, his hand was fully healed.

The pastor mentioned above commented that he was astonished to see how well the bloggers to our site access God in finding the answers to many questions that would cause great apprehension in the church that he served in. He said that coming up with the answer for this man to be reunited with his father was something for which they had not yet found an answer.

A young lady presented her problem regarding her former boy friend who began to cut his initials on her back. She was quite angry with him. Because of the amount of blood, she was concerned that her soul was somehow tied to him. She had been experiencing anger-rage that was unusual. She had not had anything to do with him in nineteen months but she could feel his anger and his moodiness and it kept her from resting. She asked how she could get free from these attacks on her soul.

A man who prays with his wife about problems on our site responded to this young lady saying that having anyone carve anything upon your body makes you an offering to Satan and places labels on you as a sucker. Specifically carving initials is often done to transfer the penalty of one's sins to another person. Because of the unforgiveness towards him, it allows not only a soul tie but also a soul attachment. In blaming him for the wrongs in her life, this young lady was triggering these ties and attachments. He counseled her to forgive him and even to stand in the gap as him, confessing his sins against her. Then he told her to stand out of the gap as herself and forgive him. Taking communion, the body and the blood of Jesus could then be taken to reject and remove the label, breaking off all effects of it, as well as rejecting being made an offering to Satan. He told her that their prayers were with her for the wisdom and the understanding to do all that was necessary to be set free from these attacks.

The same day she responded thanking him for this much needed advice. She followed the instructions of standing in the gap for him, confessing his sins, as well as thanking her heavenly Father that the stripes of Jesus had healed her. She was not only able to forgive him, but after a few minutes she could see that the scars on her back were no longer there…

The man who helped is one of our regular contributors to the blog. His answers are bathed in prayer. He shared a praise report with us saying that ordinarily he didn't speak about his past, though there were some who knew that nine years ago his spinal cord had been severed. The great news was that only last week, he began to get feeling in his feet and toes. He said that he now had feeling in the lower half of his body. And today, he could wiggle his big toe just a bit. He invited all to celebrate that his healing is here and we all complied.

All this is happening because of Jesus, because of His blood, the true understanding of His Word, the use of His name rather than the anemic title Lord, the understanding of His nine covenants presently in force, and the understanding and keeping of His days of celebration and worship.

This is also happening because people are seeking the Father's heart of love and especially of forgiveness. This book is a needed supplement to our book, *God's Fruit of Forgiveness*. The explosion of interest in the blog has highlighted the need for a frank exploration into the nitty-gritty of forgiveness, into the stark reality of what Christians face today that they didn't face fifty years ago.

We relate an amazing story involving this helpful blogger who we will call Dave, not his real name.

Dave Forgave

The man who helped the young lady is somewhat of a poster boy for the advertising of the good news of forgiveness and its explosive results. His story should encourage readers who have experienced their share of soap operatic ups and downs and struggles to forgive.

Dave and his wife came from broken homes and met and married as teens. Dave's father had not forgiven his own father and was overflowing with the distasteful and dangerous symptoms of this syndrome. He was especially abusive to his son. Dave, now in his late twenties, went to his father's home nine years ago to seek reconciliation with him.

As Dave was leaving the home, unable to achieve reconciliation, his father shot him in the back. Dave fell in a pool of blood, his spinal cord severed. Rather than calling an ambulance, Dave's dad called the police to complain that this young man was trespassing on his property. When the policeman arrived, Dave told him to tell his father that he forgave him for shooting him and for everything he had done to him during his life.

My colleague and apostle Gerald Budzinski has gained a reputation among young people on Facebook who are referred to him by friends. They see him as a man with answers who hears from God on seemingly impossible questions. Gerald was impressed with Dave's insight. He somehow managed to research his phone number and call him.

That is when Gerald learned of his amazing story and of his life now spent in a wheelchair. He asked this prayer warrior, "What do you need?" He replied simply: "All I need is more of Jesus." That's why I named one of my websites, www.robertsmoreofjesus.com.

This young man had found the secret to a successful life. It could be summed up in one phrase: Dave forgave. He learned that He could rely on His heavenly Father to give him the grace to forgive an abusive earthly father.

Dave is alive in Jesus, and even his body is coming alive in a miraculous healing.

The secret of the joy of forgiveness, and eventually reconciliation, is knowing, really knowing, the One who suffered and died for all of us, the One who said of his killers, "Father, forgive them. They don't know what they're doing."

Many of you who read these words say that you know this Jesus, who came to reveal the Father. It was the Father Himself who drew you to Jesus (John 6:44). And then Jesus chose you (John 15:16). The apostle Paul's great goal was to get to know, to really know, Jesus (Phil. 3:10).

How about us believers? Do we really know Jesus, intimately? If we did, we wouldn't be living soap opera lives filled with unforgiveness. Jesus wants us to grow up. He wants to see us mature to become like our Father Love (Mat. 5:48). But our refusal to forgive others, especially our earthly fathers, has been one of the main ways we have fallen short of the perfection of our Father.

Forgiveness has proven to be the hardest quality of our Father Love for believers to exemplify. The lack of forgiveness is the main problem in the church today.

This refusal to accept our Father's grace of forgiveness has divided families, split mates, hurt children, and made Christian lives a messy soap opera that gets bad ratings from the viewing audience of non-believers. They say, "They're no different from us, only worse! And they want us to be part of that Jesus' crowd? No way!"

The World on Our Shoulders

What they don't realize is that we're their ticket to survival. The Great Tribulation is around the corner. It will be worse than any soap opera or even horror movie we have ever seen. God calls us the salt of the earth (Mat. 5:13). Salt preserves.

Jesus describes events far more catastrophic than the horror inhabitants of Jerusalem experienced in 70 A.D.: "For then there will be great tribulation, such as has not occurred since the beginning of the world until now, nor ever will. Unless those days had been cut short, no life would have been saved; but *for the sake of the elect* those days will be cut short" (Mat. 24:21-22).

But what if the elect don't do their job? What if they don't pray and live as lights to the world and as preservers of mankind?

In our books we have explained the importance of reading the whole Bible rather than relegated what men falsely call the "Old" Testament to the dustbin. After all, Jesus did say, at a time when only that "Old Testament" existed, that we were to live by every word of God (Mat. 4:4).

You can't know who Jesus is without the First Testament, or "The First Words of Jesus," who is called the Word in John 1:1-18. And you can't fully understand the verse we have just read without Malachi 4:6.

Unless the hearts of the children are turned to their fathers and the hearts of God's children to their Father Love and to His spirit of forgiveness, Jesus will have no choice but to destroy every living thing on earth before He returns to make it fit once again for life to exist on it.

However small, a group must exist in these last days that is working for this reconciliation. Jesus is looking for a bride, His church, who is willing to obey Him, willing to keep His laws of love (John 14:15), His days, and His ways that are epitomized by the spirit of forgiveness.

Many fathers today, even Christian fathers, aren't showing love to their wives or their children because they haven't forgiven their own dads. Yet Jesus set us the example, loving His bride the church by giving of Himself for us, "so that He might sanctify her [His bride, the church], having cleansed her by the washing of water with the word" (Eph. 5:26).

Jesus cleanses our sordid past by His blood that He shed for us, and as we take the overlooked and neglected elements of communion we assure that our past is indeed washed away and that we have eternal life (John 6:53-54).

We thus assure that He lives in us. He is the personification of the grace or indwelling empowerment to obey His laws of love. When we bathe in the Word by reading it aloud, meditating on it, and practicing it, we are being cleansed and prepared as a bride for Jesus.

It's time. It's high time we got cleaned up. Many on our blog come to us with questions betraying topsy-turvy lives filled with problems, many of those problems resulting from unforgiveness, and many of them are experiencing a cleansing and a newness they haven't experienced before.

They are learning new things they have never heard in their churches, many of which have discarded them like useless rubbish because of their problems.

We welcome all of you who are in need of help, forgiveness, and reconciliation with God and man. We extend an invitation to really get to know and love Jesus, in His own words in Matthew 11:28-30: "Come to Me, all who are weary and heavy-laden [with soap opera lives more dramatically sad than they should be for believers, or perhaps even worse if you are not yet a believer], and I will give you rest. Take My yoke upon you and learn from Me, for I am gentle and humble in heart, and YOU WILL FIND REST FOR YOUR SOULS [your heart and emotions, your mind, and your will]. For My yoke is easy and My burden light."

Knowing Love

Before we get into the fascinating nitty-gritty of solving complex problems, we need to understand the basics of knowing God. He is Love (1 John 4:8). He wants all mankind to know Jesus and His salvation and live forever in the Family of Love that He heads.

Jesus gives a surprising definition of eternal life in John 17:3. He says it's knowing the Father and knowing Him. That's His purpose for us.

But oops! Lucifer and Adam used their free will God gave them, since He doesn't want robots, to rebel against Him. God is all knowing, of course, so He knew that His plan of love would require a delay before all mankind could come to Him.

Since you are reading this, you are in all likelihood one of the few He has drawn to Jesus in this age (John 6:44). The Father draws you to His Son Jesus, who died so that all your sins would be erased from the Father's memory. Then it is Jesus who chooses you because He knows you can resist Satan's onslaught in this age in which he is "god of this world" (2 Cor. 4:4).

You can then respond to His call (John 15:16), and begin to allow Him to bring about the fruits of the Father's love in your life, including the all-important grace of forgiveness. This gift enables you to forgive your physical father and mother, as well as all those who have hurt you in your life.

How important is it to know your Father Love? It is probably the most important knowledge you can possess in these last days.

In His last hours, Jesus summed up the most important thing in life: "This is eternal life, that they know You, the only true God, and Jesus Christ whom You have sent" (John 17:3). Eternal life is only available to those who truly know God, who is Love. And the degree in which we enter into the abundant life Jesus brought (John 10:10) is dependent upon how well we know Jesus.

Some who performed miracles in Jesus' name will hear these words: "I never knew you..." (Mat. 7:23). Others, who were at one point part of the virgin Bride of Jesus, will hear the words, " I do not know you" (Mat. 25:12). It is obvious that Jesus knows us who responded to His call and walk in His ways of love, knowing and loving him as demonstrated by our obedience (John 14:50). But some He ceases to know because they stopped following Him, and others He never knew.

How about you? Will Jesus say those words to you?

It's important to understand the process by which we come to know God. The Father draws you to Jesus, who is the Mediator between God the Father and mankind Jesus shed His blood for all who ever walked or will walk on the face of this earth. While many Christians believe that God the Father was the God spoken of in the Hebrew Scriptures, that's not what Jesus said.

Take your Bible and read a few verses that make this truth plain: John 1:18; 5:37; 6:46; 14:7; 17:25-26. Jesus came to reveal the Father, and He said that He was the only way to the Father (John 14:6). Mohammed and Buddha are not the way. Only Jesus is the Way, the Truth, and the Life.

Where the vast majority of Christians are confused is that they think those who don't know Jesus today, because they're not called in this age, are condemned to some fiery hell forever. That is not reflective of a God and Father who calls Himself Love, nor is it the Bible teaching. Almost seven hundred Bible verses point to a time when all who don't come to know Jesus in this age will be resurrected and offered an opportunity to know Him after His thousand-year reign on earth (Rev. 20:5a).

Cruel Tyrant, or Father Love?

If you think your Father God, who is Love, would condemn someone forever simply because He hadn't chosen to draw them to Jesus in this age, you don't know that Father Love. It's time you threw in the trash can the false conception of a cruel and distant Father who loved to smite people in the "Old Testament" and condemns innocent people willy-nilly to burn in hell forever. You may also think that, perhaps like your earthly father, He is just looking for ways to "get" you.

That's a picture of Satan, not our Father Love. If you swallow that lie, it's time to spit it out and lay it down to Jesus. Satan wants to cleverly portray Father God as the one who comes to kill, steal, and destroy rather than give His children the abundant life (John 10:10).

Are you getting the picture? Do you begin to see how Satan has deceived the whole world (Rev. 12:9), alas, even the Christian world? Do you begin to grasp how important it is for God's children to return to their true Father Love? For indeed, how can we return to our Father if we don't know who He is? Satan wants us to see our Father as the cruel scoundrel that he, the devil, is. He even wants you see yourself as a dirty, rotten scoundrel of a sinner who is unworthy of the Father's love.

But that's not who you are if you have accepted Jesus as your Savior and Divine Master. If you have Jesus living in you, that means that the real you, your spirit man, has been washed perfectly clean by Jesus' blood. Your past has been washed away along with all your sins so that you can come boldly before the throne of your Father (Heb. 4:16) and get to know Him.

The doctrines of the Christian world are full of falseness. Our Father Love has gotten bad press in the pulpits of churchianity. If we persist in that falseness, our hearts can't return to our Father in heaven, or even to our earthly fathers.

Our bloggers who began to recognize their unforgiveness to their physical fathers let out a common cry: "We need Jesus!" The man we call Dave, who forgave his father for shooting him in the back when he came back for a hug, said, " I need more of Jesus." We all do.

We need Jesus, because in knowing Him we get to know our Father.

Does your heart yearn to truly know Jesus? Is your heart feeling a tug from the Holy Spirit to get to know your Father Love and turn to Him in these last days?

You've come to the right place, to a place where God is restoring lost truths, truths whose light chases away the darkness of falseness that has swallowed up the world (Isa. 25:7)—truths that will set your heart free to embrace the unconditional love of the Father.

Are you ready for Love? Are you ready to allow the light of God's truth to shine on the darkness of your life? Perhaps you have a life and a family that has been ravaged by Satan's sad soap operas. It's not too late to receive God's love and change your life.

Isaiah tells us to seek the Eternal while He may be found (55:6). Some of our troubled bloggers have found hope and freedom, a hope God offers to you: " For you will go out with joy and be led forth with peace; The mountains and the hills will break forth into shouts of joy before you, and all the trees of the field will clap their hands. Instead of the thorn bush [symbolic of demons] the cypress will come up, And instead of the nettle the myrtle will come up…" (Isa. 55:12-13).

Your Father hasn't come to abuse you like your earthly father may have done. His plans for you are "for welfare and not for calamity and to give you a future and a hope" (Jer. 29:11). Yes, as we approach the most calamitous times in the history of civilization, these can be the most exciting times for you and your family. Nothing is more exciting than getting to know Love, loving and obeying a Father who is eagerly waiting in these last days to wrap you in His arms of protective love.

God promises to those who love and seek Jesus in these last days that not a *hair* of your head will perish (Luke 21:18). That means you don't have to allow your head to be cut off by ISIS. The precursors to the Islamic Antichrist plan to do their scandalous deeds, faithful to the words of their Koran, to believers in the West. But you don't have to be their victims if you know Jesus, who He is and who you are in Him.

Even if you don't qualify for the first rapture, the one to heaven, God promises that He will protect you if you have tasted how good He is. Psalm 31:19-20 tells us, "How great is Your goodness, which You have stored up for those who [revere] You, which You have wrought for those who take refuge in You before the sons of men [including the Islamic terrorists the U.S. government refuses to call what they are]. You hide them in the secret place of Your presence from the conspiracies of man; You keep them secretly in a shelter from the strife of tongues."

Our Father is a God of great loving kindness and mercy. He rewards those who seek Him with all their hearts. You need have no fear as others, including Christians, receive the horrible circumstances that they fear. No fear exists in those who abide in the secret place of Father Love. But how do we get to know the Father?

Know the Son, Know the Father

Jesus told His religious foes, "… if you knew Me, you would know My Father also" (John 8:19). So why don't we start there?

A popular religious deception goes like this: sweet Jesus came to set us free from the impossible-to-keep, picky laws of His harsh and cruel Father who was the God who loved to smash the smithereens out of people in the Old Testament. Maybe you've never heard it put quite that way, but that is the clear impression you get from hearing the messages from our pulpits today.

And what images are you bombarded with to give you a picture of who Jesus was when he walked the earth? While long hair does not always equal an effeminate nature, God plainly tells us that it is a shame for man to have long hair (1 Cor. 11:14). That may be a detail, but it is part of the deceptive picture Satan has painted of our Jesus. With the exception of the visions in *Heaven is for Real,* in pictures and movies, Jesus is portrayed as a longhaired, weak, effeminate man, and many churches today are even portraying a gay Jesus who leaned against His lover John.

This is utter nonsense. Yet believers have some of these ideas in the back of their minds as they are thinking about the Father and Jesus. And we must not forget the third member of the Godhead, our Comforter, Teacher, and Governor of the earth, the Holy Spirit, who is also God.

This brings us to the important question: who and what is God? God or the Hebrew *Elohim* is a Family of spirit beings (except the resurrected Jesus appears as a man with a glorified body beside the Father in heaven], a family whose name is Love. Only the " top brass," for lack of a better term, the Triune Godhead, are in the strictest sense of the term *Yahovah,* or the Eternal One, the united Threesome who have always existed and who brought all things and all beings into existence. God created mankind in order to form members of that divine Family of Love.

We do indeed become one with the Eternal One, and thus dwell in the eternal realm with Him. We aren't, however, part of the Triune Godhead of which each Member bears the name *Yahovah.* We could say we are eternal ones under the authority of the three Beings who have always existed and whom we worship. Those three Beings are one *Elohim,* one Godhead who are *echad* (Deut. 6:4), One in the sense of being perfectly united in character and purpose, not one Personage or Personality.

Knowing the Father begins by knowing Jesus, since no man can come to the Father but through Him (John 14:6).

Knowing Jesus as God

Satan has done all he can to block the understanding of our awesome purpose. He has used many schemes, but one seemingly small one has caused great misunderstanding. The venerated King James Bible produced some issues that are far less than venerable.

Our Eternal God has a bigger picture of Himself than what is painted by the use of an English term of nobility extant in 1611. While differing with the popular notion that Jesus is Lord may seem anathema to many, we have amply shown in our writings the truth about the unfortunate and even diabolical mistranslation "Lord" made popular in large part by the King James Bible.

Did you know that this term of nobility was five to seven levels below the title of king? Did you know that God calls Satan "the god of this world" (2 Cor. 4:4)? Kings are higher in authority, much higher, than lords. In the history of Israel, priests represented God and thus possessed a higher authority than kings. Priests represented the highest authority, supreme authority of heaven, whereas kings exercised civil authority as they ideally responded to the inspiration of the priesthood, with their direct heavenly contact.

If Satan is the god of this world, and Jesus is a lord far below the authority of even a king, what does that mean? Followed to its conclusion, it would mean that Jesus is under Satan. That is why it's so important to emphasize that Jesus is God, not a lowly lord, notwithstanding all the wrong translations that have confused the Christian world. Satan has succeeded in this clever way to hide from us our awesome identity as gods on the earth under the authority of the Supreme Godhead.

In the same way that some will accuse us of blasphemy, the Jews thought Jesus was blaspheming when Jesus declared Himself God. If you read attentively John 10:32-36 and Psalm 82:6, you'll see that Jesus declared that mankind was called also to be *Elohim* or Gods under the

Most High God on the earth. What God said to Adam in Genesis 1:26-27 dispels the weak arguments about the Hebrew word only meaning physical judges.

How can you realize your amazing destiny if you think Jesus was only a lowly lord way below a king? You are called to be like your Father in heaven and to rule with Him forever, so why relegate Jesus to a position lower than you, or even Satan? Think about it.

You can't know who you are in Jesus if you don't know who Jesus is? And you can't know Him unless you read and understand the whole Bible. You cannot even believe what Jesus said in His New Testament if you don't believe His words in the First Testament. We didn't make that up. Jesus said in John 5:47, "But if you do not believe his [Moses'] writings, how will you believe My words?"

How can you live by every word of God (Mat. 4:4) if you don't read and meditate on every part of the Word of God?

How can you fight Satan with the Sword of the Word if you only have one-fourth of a sword, since the First Testament is virtually three-fourths of the Bible?

Furthermore, did you realize that it was Jesus, not the Father, who did all that smiting in the First Testament? Maybe you don't know Jesus like you think you know Him. Remember, He's the One who, along with taking the children tenderly in His arms, also took a whip and chased the merchants out of His Father's house as He, the supposedly weak wimp, overthrew six-hundred-pound tables. Some wimp! He was a man's man, a carpenter who was strong physically and spiritually.

The Real Jesus Means Business

You may think Jesus came to do away with His Father's law and bring in that vague definition of love that allows so much confusion in the church today. But Jesus was no pushover. He is the God who will not be mocked. He is the God who says that unless you obey Him, you don't love Him (John 14:15), and you surely don't know Him.

We in this Laodicean era of the church need to know the real Jesus who gives us a stern warning: "So because you are lukewarm, and neither hot nor cold, I will spit you out of My mouth" (Rev. 3:16). Jesus is not some namby-pamby weakling, and He doesn't want us to be like that either. But we can only be strong as we know Him and allow Him to be the Grace in us that overcomes the world (John 16:33). He says that apart from Him we can do nothing (John 15:5).

Our God wants to present us blameless as the Bride of Jesus, and "He also will bring it to pass" (1 Thes. 5:23-24). God tells us in Psalm 46:10, "Cease striving [or be still] and know that I am God…" He wants us to know that He is the One who sanctifies us or makes us holy like Him (Ex. 31:13).

How Much Does the Flesh Profit?

You would think Christians and especially pastors would easily be able to answer the question, "How much does the flesh profit?" But Christians on Freedom Blog have cited pastors and others who seem to think the phrase, "God helps those who help themselves," is in the Bible. It's not. Nor is the principle it expresses.

While bloggers have cited various verses taken out of context to try to prove their point that we must go to the limit of our power before God will help us, the simple answer is stated by Jesus and is supported by other verses.

Have some longtime believers overlooked some important basic teachings and even neglected to start at the starting points God decrees? Otherwise, how can we explain such ignorance, such destructive lack of knowledge (Hos. 4:6)?

Maybe we've missed the part about surrendering to Jesus? Maybe many have not heeded the *command* to be baptized if we want to truly be saved (Acts 2:38; Mark 16:16)? Is that why some of us insist on putting more emphasis on works in our own fleshly strength rather than relying on Jesus?

We're sure a number of reasons explain why we Christians look to the flesh more than the spirit. Fear is one of them.

Since September 11, 2001, fear has gripped the world, even the Christian world. Satan attacks, and what do we do? We often panic. We run to the phone, not the throne. We seek worldly solutions because we don't know what to do. We don't know what to do because our fear keeps us from going to God for the solutions.

False doctrine is another reason, and not knowing who we are in Jesus, both resulting from not knowing who Jesus is, which the First Testament explains. If you think God is a cruel, distant tyrant, you're not going to want to go to Him for solutions, are you? Knowing God begins by surrendering to Jesus and obeying Him (John 14:15; Ps. 111:10).

What is one of the best ways to continue that knowing process?

We get to know authors by the words they write. We get to know God by reading, studying, and meditating on His Book. Even pastors don't tend nowadays to read the Bible. They read ready-made sermon scripts provided for them, but few actually ask the Holy Spirit to teach them the Word of God, as the man after the Father's heart did (Ps. 119:18).

How can our hearts return to our Father Love if we don't read His heart in His Word?

You're waiting, however, for the answer to our question, "How much does the flesh profit?" Jesus gives the answer: "It is the Spirit who gives life; the flesh profits nothing; the words that I have spoken to you are spirit and are life" (John 6:63).

It's settled. Jesus didn't say, "You work as hard as you can in your fleshly strength, and when I see how hard you are toiling, then I will come and see you through." He didn't say, "The flesh profits a certain amount."

He didn't say, as one theological professor paraphrased John 15:5, "Apart from Me you can do nothing of lasting value."

No. He said, "The flesh profits *nothing*." He said, "…apart from Me you can do *nothing*" (John 15:5).

God is the One who does His works in and through us (Ps. 57:2; Phil. 4:13). Until we understand that, we are spiritual infants.

Even seasoned believers, of course, fall into works of the flesh at times, but they get back on track quickly. In our Freedom Blog we for a short time began to think how we in our flesh could make our blog a success, rather than relying on God to make it a success. We got quickly back on track, and we encourage you, if you have resorted to fleshly, worldly ways, to repent as we did and "cease striving" in the flesh, or be still, knowing that God is working through you, and He is in charge (Ps. 46:10). The only help He needs from us is our submission to Him and our recognition that He will do the works in and through us.

Who Does the Works?

"Oh," but some will say, "God says we are to work out our own salvation." Does the Bible say that?

Here is that verse in context: "…work out your salvation with [awe and reverence]; for it is *God* who is at work in you, both to will and to work for His good pleasure. Do all things without grumbling or disputing…" (Phil. 2:12b-14). Notice that it is God who is doing the works in and through us as we submit to Him. Does it take cooperation, a partnership? Yes, of course.

That partnership, however, is based on our surrender to God so He can do the works in us. How else could we do all things without grumbling? It's His grace or empowerment. Jesus is the Grace within us that empowers us to grow to be more like our Father and have His heart of love.

The apostle Paul combats the false idea that we must be justified with our Father by our fleshly efforts to keep God's law of love. He says that we conquer sin, the breaking of the law (1 John 3:4), because we are under grace, the favor and supernatural empowerment of God in us (Rom. 6:14; Titus 2:11-12). Our righteousness isn't based on keeping any law but by the blood of Jesus and His life in us (Rom. 5:9-10).

Paul said, "...for we are the true circumcision, who worship in the Spirit of God and glory in Christ Jesus and put no confidence in the flesh..." (Phil. 3:3). Paul went on to explain how he, of all people, could claim that confidence, being a Jew of Jews and student of the eminent Gamaliel. But he said he counted "all things to be loss in view of the surpassing value of knowing Jesus Christ my [Divine Master]..." (Phil. 3:8).

No value, indeed, surpasses the awesome privilege of knowing Jesus, who opens to us the inestimable value of knowing our Father and the Holy Spirit. Paul's great ambition was expressed in verse 10: "...that I may know Him..." Is that our great desire? That was the one thing David desired (Psalm 27:4), and if we want to be men and women after God's own heart, that should be our desire.

The Secret of Knowing Jesus

David knew the secret of knowing Jesus and getting to know Him more and more. What made him a man after God's own heart? And what will make us in these last days men and women who truly know Jesus and know and follow the Father's heart of love? What will cause our hearts to turn back to our Father?

We have already mentioned the need to accept and surrender to Jesus, as epitomized by water baptism (Rom. 6:1-14). As we continue to deepen our surrender, we become baptized or immersed in a spiritual sense in Jesus and the Holy Spirit. And that process begins by putting our triune nature in the right order, spirit, soul (mind, heart, and will), and body.

The real David, his spirit man, spoke to his soul and will so that his entire essence, including his body, would come in line with the Holy Spirit who guided his spirit. Psalm 103 gives us an example of how he spoke to his will.

David said, "Bless [Jesus], O my soul, and all that is within me, bless His holy name." Every day David made declarations to his soul to line up with the will of the Father in heaven as revealed through the

God with whom he was intimate, Jesus (Ps. 110:1). He told his soul to line up with his spirit. At www.freedomchurchofgod.com we have given suggestions for declarations of our identity and intention to obey based on the Word of God. We must set our priorities as we begin each day.

"Bless [Jesus]," David continued, "O my soul, and forget none of His benefits…" We tend to dwell on our problems rather than on the God who is bigger than our problems. We speak about the mountain facing us rather than speaking to the mountain. Dwelling on the blessings and the covenant promises God has given us will transform our attitude to one of thanksgiving, a powerful practice that releases even more blessings.

Our words have great power, especially when combined with an attitude of thanksgiving. Gary Keesee, presenter on TV's *Fixing the Money Thing,* shows us how our words affect our finances. An avid hunter, he spotted a $2000 gun that was just what he wanted, but since he didn't feel like paying that at the time, he simply pointed to it, claimed it, and thanked the Father for it. A short time afterwards, after he spoke to a business group, the host presented him with a gift on behalf of the group. He told no one about his gesture, but they blessed him with the exact gun he had claimed.

David, a man who saw his adultery/murder erased, spoke out his gratitude for God's extravagant forgiveness (verse 3a). Do we thank God regularly for forgiving us when we have also fallen? He gives us the grace to get up and forgets every one of our sins upon confession (Micah 7:7-8, 18-19; Heb. 8:12; 1 John 1:9). If we accept it, He gives us a "righteousness consciousness" rather than "consciousness of sins" (Heb. 10:2). We have the awesome privilege of turning over to Jesus all our sins and burdens. We don't have to accept any of Satan's gifts (Ex. 6:7; Ps. 55:22; 1 Pet. 5:7; Mat. 11:28-30).

David reminded his soul and body that Jesus had healed all his diseases (verse 3b). When you truly know Jesus, you know you are healed (1 Pet. 2:24). If some unknown hindrances delay the manifestation of that healing, you know God will reveal that which blocks the healing. When you don't know Jesus, you don't know you are healed. One of our bloggers, trapped for the time being in a wheelchair, told our apostle he knew he was healed, and soon thereafter he began to get feeling in his legs, an impossibility in the natural realm.

David knew his life was redeemed from the pit (Ps. 103:4). Do you know that? When you know Jesus, you know that Satan cannot hold you in any pit or rut into which you may fall. You concentrate on where you are in Jesus, in heaven looking down on Satan, who belongs in the pit (Eph. 2:6).

When you put the accent on where you are in Jesus, in the heavenly places, God has a reason to rapture you out of the evil of these last days (Luke 21:36). Your spirit man comes first (1 Thes. 5:23), and you're used to being caught up into heaven, so you will soon be literally, spirit, soul, and body in heaven as you prepare to come down and rule with Jesus (Rev. 5:10).

You are redeemed by Jesus' blood because your Father loves you. You know it, and you "say so" (Ps. 107:2)—often. Satan can't hold you in any pit, since you know who you are in Jesus, and you regularly send him and his demons to the pit where *they* belong, not you (Col. 2:15; 1 John 3:8; 4:4).

Knowing Jesus Crowns You with Loving Kindness

David blessed the God who "crowns you with lovingkindness and compassion" (Ps. 103:4). As you grow from being a child of God to a mature son (Rom. 6:14; Heb. 5:12-14), you are ready to wear the cloak of glory (Ps. 68:34; John 17:22; Rom. 8:17, 29-30) and exercise authority as if you were Jesus Himself, since He lives in you. This sends shivers through Satan's spineless, cowardly being (1 John 4:17; James 2:19). When you know who you are, Satan can't tell you apart from Jesus. He only sees Jesus' light in you that causes his darkness to tremble.

The crown of loving kindness includes the ability to:

- Forgive and grant freedom from sin and its consequences (John 20:23; 2 Cor. 5:18-21).
- Grant yourself and others a brand new start (2 Cor. 4:16; John 8:11).

- Grant friendship to one in great spiritual need (Gal. 6:1-2).
- Come into oneness with the Father (John 17:23).
- Be patient with others and their shortcomings (1 Cor. 13:4-7).
- Teach others God-given boundaries.
- Speak life into another's soul (as did a prayer warrior on our blog, speaking life into souls deadened by unforgiveness).

The crown of compassion includes some of the above, as well as loving the unlovable, binding and removing demons to release troubled souls, removing Satan's weapons, blessing rather than cursing, declaring healing to the body and soul of another, praying for people and seeing them healed, and using wisdom to help others.

David thanked Jesus in Psalm 103:5, "Who satisfies your years with good things..." As we seek Jesus, His kingdom, and His righteousness first in our lives (Mat. 6:33), we open the door for the Father of love and light to shine on us and give us every good and perfect gift (James 1:17).

When knowing Jesus is our priority, all God's promises are released to us as we claim them and realize we are worthy of them because of Jesus. Long and abundant life is ours (Ps. 91:16; John 10:10), and our youth is renewed (Ps. 103:5b).

When Satan steps in to try to oppress us, Jesus performs righteous deeds and justice for us (Ps. 103:6; 146:7). Satan is stepping up his plan to oppress Israel (the believers) and the sons of Judah (those who praise Jesus), but our Redeemer is stronger than Satan and will contend for us (Jer. 50:33-34).

We must, however, speak God's Word into our souls. As we recognize His character as expressed in Psalm 103:8-19, we can grow to be like Him. We must first, however, know what He is like, speaking those parts of the Word that express His character into our hearts and minds. We can then have our hearts turned to the heart of love of our Father. The simple choice to obey is a key (Ps. 103:18).

CHAPTER 2

What's Keeping You from Knowing Jesus?

J esus knows us perfectly and intimately, and He wants us to know Him the same way. But Satan has put up a wall of confusion to try to keep us from truly knowing the One who died for us. The art of getting to know Jesus is not that complicated, but Satan has created confusion to make knowing Jesus extremely difficult. But you can.

Paul was concerned for the Corinthians that Satan by his craftiness would cause their minds to be "led astray from the simplicity and purity of devotion to Christ" (2 Cor. 11:3). An "undistracted devotion to [Jesus]" (1 Cor. 7:35) seems to be the exception today in our fast-paced society.

What about you? Are you caught in Satan's web of confusion that keeps you from really getting to know Jesus? Below are some examples of why some of us may not be getting to know Jesus:

- *A willingness to declare ourselves bored.* We might say things like: "I am so tired of coming to church, reading the Bible, praying…" The origin of the word *bored* comes from the idea of boring a hole in your head and draining off the life force and "dumbing yourself down." Being bored implies also being dumb. As a teen if we said, "This is so boring," we need to rescind in Jesus' name that phrase and every word in which we have declared boredom over our life.

- *A desire to avoid studying, learning, or taking time to pray.* It is so easy to fall into this trap of starving your soul. When we let the important things slide, we start on a downhill slope to utter spiritual laziness and a confused life.

- *An openness to all distractions.* A distraction is anything that keeps us from our priority time with God. They could include television, phone calls, people, emails, social media time, or computer games. Little foxes ruin the vineyards (Song of Solomon 2:15) and little bits of leaven or sin leaven the whole lump (1 Cor. 5:6). The little breach can widen gradually like a wall whose "collapse comes suddenly in an instant" (Isa. 30:13). Too easily we become like Martha, "worried and bothered about so many things" (Luke 10:41-42) in the kitchen while Jesus is waiting for us in the living room. We need the wisdom to know when "one thing is necessary," and that is quiet time with our heavenly Father. Declaring to our will and soul that we will not be moved by distractions when we know we need time alone with God is the best way to keep our focus. See what the "one thing" was that David wanted in Psalm 27:4.

- *Proclivity to daydream.* When we let our minds wander into fleshly, lustful, or prideful thoughts and fantasies, we are not on the road to getting to know Jesus. These wanderings can become strongholds or evil spiritual fortresses. As policemen will sometimes speak the code 10-4, meaning they understand the message from their boss, we need to understand loud and clear another 10-4: "For the weapons of our warfare are not of the flesh, but divinely powerful for the destruction of fortresses" (2 Cor. 10:4). We are to take "every thought captive to the obedience of Christ" (verse 5).

- *A reliance on panic for solutions to a problem.* What do we do when a problem arises? Do we throw our hands in the air in desperation and speak words of panic? Or do we go to our Father and pray for guidance, giving the problem to

Jesus for redemption and a solution? Speaking negativity into the situation is cursing, which is a panic response, and panic activates the spirit of fear, causing loss of contact with Jesus, the One who can rescue us. We have commanded the Holy Spirit to stand back and invited fear to rule. In those times we need to be reminded that we can be "afflicted in every way, but not crushed; perplexed, but not despairing" (2 Cor. 4:8). We often forget that the One who lives in us has given us His peace, and He tells us, "In the world you have tribulation, but take courage; I have overcome the world" (John 16:33).

- *Letting anger/rage flare before being ready to listen to instructions.* One blogger who had not forgiven his father would not listen to instructions from God's Word. He said we were twisted and evil because we think God gives us all the answers. He said he would get even with his dad and with us. His anger/rage and refusal to listen are easy to see. Some who go far into unforgiveness make God in *their* image, thinking they hear from Him, and often making gods of themselves.

- *A self-cursing approach to setbacks, losses, and minor failures.* Phrases like, "I'm just not meant to succeed. I was born to fail," are curses against ourselves. They give the demons legal right to attack, even with physical sickness.

- *Establishing television, games, or addictions to take our minds off growth and change.* When we know we have something important to do, and instead we flee to addictions, these distracting pursuits steal our growth and motivation. But taking time with Jesus and turning these addictions over to Jesus can produce dramatic results. A young blogger wrote in to say that he had been addicted to crack cocaine for over twelve years. He was only twenty-one. He decided to keep the Sabbath as his day of freedom. During that time, he turned the addiction over to Jesus as well as all the unforgiveness. It has been a month and he is totally free. He is so thankful that Jesus takes such problems. When the readers of our blog realize they need Jesus, to know Him more intimately, Jesus responds with miracles.

- *Coveting a blanket of squandering.* Simply put, squandering is wasting our time, money, or energy in non-priority pursuits. Most often the cause is receiving into our hearts false labels put upon us. The root is often selfishness and the blanket can be based on the spirit of anger/rage, which invites high blood pressure and more squandering. Many churches are affected by this blanket, which stops God's blessings.
- *Acting on our fears, dreads, and lusts.* Sin cuts us off from Jesus (Isa. 59:1-3) and from getting to know Him. "You cannot drink the cup of [Jesus] and the cup of demons…" (1 Cor. 10:21).
- *Painting ourselves into debt, obligations, and promises we cannot keep.* Such actions activate the spirit of confusion. God tells us to say yes or no (Mat. 5:37) and mean it. Sometimes, in order to protect our boundaries, we need to say no to certain people and requests.
- *An ability to lose or misplace things or to dispose of learning materials when we need them.* This problem is sometimes caused by unforgiveness and anger/rage blocking our brain/mind connection. In many cases we are listening to the god of confusion rather than the Holy Spirit.

Words That Keep Us from Knowing Jesus

This last category of confusion that keeps us from knowing Jesus can be brought on by the words we speak, words that bring on easy loss. Here are some phrases we must turn over to Jesus and rescind as we turn over the other areas of confusion:

- "I forgot. I just keep forgetting these things."
- "I would lose my head if it weren't screwed on." These words also can lead to perversions and addictions.
- "I can't seem to find anything." Did we pray about what we need to find?

- "I can't seem to win for losing." Jesus says we are winners, victors, more than conquerors (Rom. 8:37; 1 Cor. 15:57; 2 Cor. 2:14). Why invite failure and loss?
- "This is like beating a dead dog or dead horse." A pastor spoke this over a church because they weren't giving enough money, and the church fell apart.
- "I will never understand this." We are declaring we want Satan to steal our understanding of the Word of God.
- "All good things come to those who sit and wait, so I guess I will just have to sit here and wait." Jesus commanded us to work six days of the week and rest on the seventh. Such words will cause us to lose all blessings of creativity, our walk with God, and the blessings of Jesus. While we don't toil as Adam did after sin entered, we are to produce increase by sowing seeds in productive work.
- "My brain can't handle any more." The Bible repeatedly says not to limit God or ourselves, since we can do all things in Jesus (Phil. 4:13) and have His mind, thoughts, and attitudes (1 Cor. 2:16; Phil. 2:5).
- "I'm glad somebody knows what is going on." Are we only following the leader, refusing to accept the truth that we have the capacity to know all things in Jesus (Col. 2:3)?
- "I hate doing things like that." Unless we're talking about sin, we are limiting ourselves by such words, an example of which would be, "I hate tithing; God is stealing from me." We thus block our blessing.
- "This job just isn't for me." Why would we block our advancement and promotion rather than giving thanks to God for where we are as we call on Him for promotion or a new and better job? How can we be surrounded with favor as with a shield (Ps. 5:12) if we are putting up a shield to block the favor by our words?
- "I don't know about that." Instead of looking into a new Bible understanding we hear in order to "examine everything" and hold fast to the truth (1 Thes. 5:21), we invite Satan to destroy

us through lack of knowledge (Hos. 4:6) and make it so the truth will never find a home in our hearts and minds. We cling to our traditions rather than studying a new belief that God wants us to incorporate into our minds and lives (Mark 7:7-8). We are claiming ignorance rather than being enriched in God's knowledge (1 Cor. 1:5). We are called to walk in God's wisdom and to understand His will (Eph. 5:15-17).

These open doors to Satan allow him to block our understanding of the Word and allow him to steal the Word we receive (Mat. 13:19). We know Jesus through His Word, so why would we allow Satan to block the sowing of the Word seed into our hearts?

Wild Paris Driving and the Spirit of Diversion

Satan has another method of keeping us from knowing Jesus. He uses the spirit of diversion to divert us from what is important.

In 1984 I was called to preach a sermon on the Day of Atonement in Paris, France. Satan tried to divert us from our mission. He had incited Jew haters to bomb a synagogue in Paris, which caused an unexpected deviation from the normal route to the Eiffel Tower area where we held services. However, the wild Paris driving abilities I had used when I lived there in the early seventies came back. I didn't drive like Bourne in the movie *The Bourne Identity,* but I was not driving like an American. Our daughter of four said, "Oh, Daddy, this is fun. It's like a roller coaster!"

The good news is that all my traffic sins are forgiven, and that we made it to the church on time. All too often we do not do as well when it comes to Satan's efforts to divert us from our purpose on a daily basis.

The devil uses his spirit of diversion to make us miss our prayer time and seeking direction from God on what He wants us to do daily. We lose sound reasoning as we are diverted into emotionalism, compromise, and lying. We start redoing our past, getting stuck there. These emotional reactions can easily become habitual and make it hard for us to return to our first love and zeal for Jesus. We become fearful of truly getting to know Jesus.

How do we avoid these diversions, these wrong words, and these weapons of Satan to bring confusion into our lives? How do we follow Jesus' example of single-mindedness? How do we direct our hearts "into the love of God and the steadfastness of Christ," who said, "I have set my face like flint, And I know that I will not be ashamed" (Isa. 50:7)?

We must put our spirit man first. We must make declarations out loud, speaking to our wills and our souls, starting our day with declarations of who we are in Jesus. David spoke to his will and soul. Read and meditate on Psalm 103 to see how he did it.

When we realize that we are in the heavenly places with Jesus (Eph. 2:6; Col. 3:1-4; Rev. 12:12), we become accustomed to our heavenly home. The rapture will come easily, since we are already used to dwelling in heaven with Jesus where no enemy causes us fear. We know Love, and no fear dwells in Love. As our hearts are turned to our Father Love, we can be confident that in these turbulent last days, no evil will befall us (Psalm 91:1-16) under the shadow of God's wings of protection and love.

CHAPTER 3

Malachi 4:6—The Overview

M any believers, even pastors, understand a verse a certain way, and they believe that's the only way. God is not that limited. The Bible is like a multifaceted diamond that shines in different ways. Each Bible verse has at least four meanings.

Malachi 4:6 refers to family forgiveness and restoration. It also refers to the hearts of God's children returning to Father Love in the last days. It refers to the hearts of pastoral fathers returning to love God's children, and their hearts returning to those revived pastors. Last, it refers to the unity of the Hebrew fathers to the children, believers in Jesus, including the believers returning to the roots of the Hebrew and biblical "olive tree" (Rom. 11:17), the anointing, teaching, and practice of the Hebrew Scripture.

The Olive Tree

We refer to the Judeo-Christian ethic, meaning that the Christian world came from the Hebrew Bible. One meaning of fathers is that the fathers are the Hebrew people and the children are the Christians.

Already messages of warning are being given to the nation of Israel or Judah. This was prophesied in Isaiah 40:9. Many Jews will respond and accept Jesus. Christians are known to be the best friends of Israel in the world. The fathers and the children are indeed getting together.

Much more is involved, however. More and more Christians are speaking of their Jewish roots, which in reality are the biblical roots. In most cases, Christians are only taking a smattering of the biblical roots, taking the Seder or Passover as more of a cute thing rather than truly obeying God by keeping the feasts His way.

Paul speaks of these biblical roots in Romans 11:29. He says that the Gentiles "became partaker with them of the rich root of the olive tree." That rich root is the whole Hebrew Bible, the First Testament, and all the laws Jesus gave to Israel, the believers, except the laws of sacrifices and rituals that were done away during a time of reformation as Jesus sacrificed Himself (Hebrews 9:10).

Jesus told us to live by every word of God (Matthew 4:4). That includes the laws of love in the Hebrew Bible. They include the Sabbath Jesus said to remember (Ex. 20:8) and the holy days of Leviticus 23. The last days Church is pictured as a church that keeps the commandments of God (Revelation 12:17). Some will return to the Sabbath covenant, thus fulfilling this part of Malachi 4:6.

For the most part the church has denigrated the words of Jesus by calling the First Testament the "*Old* Testament," a title given by men. They have thus missed the richness of the olive root. That root is Jesus, the Anointed One. He spoke all the words of the Bible, not merely those of the New Testament.

Most of the first Christians were Jews, who kept the holy days mentioned in Leviticus 23. In fact, that's how the church got started, meeting in unity, keeping the Feast or First Fruits or Pentecost in Acts 2. Had there been no obedience or respect of biblical roots, there would've been no church, no Holy Spirit descending. God gives His Spirit to those who obey him (Acts 5:32).

Many of the practices Jesus began in the New Testament actually had roots in Hebrew practice, including baptism. We see in Leviticus 6:16 that the priests were to eat part of the sacrifice. And who did the sacrifice represent? Jesus. So Jesus told His disciples in John 6 that unless they ate of Him, they had no life.

The arguments that Gentiles had in the first century about the Jewishness of the olive tree did not involve the laws of God in the First

Testament, but circumcision. New Covenant circumcision involves baptism and especially the new moons, the turning over of spiritual uncleanness to Jesus in the same manner in which physical circumcision removed physical uncleanness.

Whose Mark Will You Take?

One of the most important aspects of the richness of the olive tree is the Sabbath day. Some are teaching that Jesus emphasized the law because He was under the Old Covenant when He spoke, and that once He died and was resurrected, a new gospel of grace taught by Paul did away the need for the Ten Commandments.

Paul, however, said to follow him as he followed Jesus (1 Cor. 11:1), and he believed and taught obedience to the same laws in the Old Covenant (Acts 24:14; 1 Cor. 7:19; Acts 13:42). The disciples kept the Sabbath commandment after Jesus died (Luke 23:56).

We follow Jesus by following His Word. I encourage you to open up your Bibles and to read aloud every verse that we quote as proof in parentheses. They are included so that you can examine all things according to the Word (I Thes. 5:21). I will always point you to the Word, and I encourage you not to believe me but to believe God's Word.

Jesus said we would know we are His disciples because of His love in us (John 13:35). Another important sign will reappear in the last days, just as Satan's mark will also appear. It's a matter that is insignificant for Christians today, but it is extremely important to God: which days you keep. Jesus speaks of His Sabbaths (plural) as a sign between Him and His people so that we may know who He is and who we are in Him (Ex. 31:13).

If believers ever bothered to compare Revelation 13 and Exodus 13, they would understand. In speaking of the spring holy days as symbolic of all His days, Jesus said they would be a sign on your forehead (your mind) and your hand (your actions or will). That's in Exodus 13:9. Eerily similar is the mark of the Beast, a mark "in their right hand and on their forehead" (Rev. 13:16). It may include a chip in our hand and forehead, but that chip will only be on those who have the biblical mark, Sunday keeping.

If the sign of God is represented by the Sabbath and holy days, it would be obvious that Satan's end-time mark would be his days, days never found in the Bible but ordained by the pope and followed by most Christians today. Jesus never ordained Sunday, Christmas, and Easter.

Satan would allow the pope's protesting daughters to protest all they wanted, but he made sure they didn't protest Sunday. The root of Sunday worship is that the Protestants don't really want to dethrone the pope as the "vicar of Christ" or the replacement of Jesus on earth. Satan still has them hooked on Sunday so he can bring them back to the Catholic fold in the last days (Isa. 47:8; 23:15-17). That is happening before our very eyes!

You can't have your heart turned to the Father if you're keeping Satan's day. The day will come soon when you have a choice. The Sabbath will be revealed, and those who at that time say no to the sign of God will automatically accept the mark of the Beast.

If we don't accept God's Sabbath rest reserved for His people (Heb. 4:9-11), we will have no rest with Satan's days and ways, even though we may be able to buy and sell. This day Jesus made for man as a sign for His end-time people will be a huge test (Mark 2:27-28; Ex. 16:4, 31:13; Rev. 12:17). Will you pass?

It's the end-time test of love. Jesus said if we loved Him, we would keep His commandments. And if we break one, when aware of it (James 4:17), we break them all (James 2:10). Food for thought: do you trust Jesus for food and protection, or do you trust the Beast? Whose mark will you take?

CHAPTER 4

Unforgiveness and the Father-hating Syndrome

Have you forgiven everyone who has hurt you in your life? Think about it. This would be a good time to take one of those "selahs" (pauses to meditate) found in the Psalms.

Can't think of anyone? Are you sure?

The Bondage Breaker author Neil Anderson said on a Christian talk show that he believed, as we do, that unforgiveness is one of the most, if not the most prevalent problem in the church today. Yes, that's in the church, the group that is supposed to show the world who God is, Love (1 John 4:8).

The apostle Paul echoed the criteria Jesus gave to prove we loved Him, which is keeping His commandments of love (John 14:15). Paul said it didn't matter whether you were Jew or Gentile. What mattered was keeping the commandments of God, who is Love (1 Cor. 7:19) and walking in "faith working through love" (Gal. 5:6). No wonder Jesus wondered if He would find faith on earth in the last days (Luke 18:8).

He knew that the law would be under attack. He prophesied that lawlessness would abound, and the result will be that "most people's love will grow cold" and only the believers who endure to the end in the ways of love will be finally saved (Mat. 24:13-14).

All this kind of makes you wonder also about that verse in John 13:35: "By this all men will know that you are My disciples, if you love one another." Refusing to forgive another believer or a non-believer isn't love, is it?

And how can we forgive others if we have not forgiven our Father in heaven. It doesn't matter that He is perfect. Many of us still can't understand why He has allowed so much pain in our lives.

We are taught in many of our churches that He is an old ogre, a cruel, capricious Father who loved to smite people in "that Old Testament," but Jesus saved the day, coming to undo all those harsh laws and treat people with love rather than being on their case all the time. We will debunk that lie in this book.

We must ask ourselves a question, however: Why did our Father, who inspired Malachi 4:6 through the Holy Spirit, prophesy that the hearts of the children would need to return to the *fathers*, not the mothers?

Could the One who says He knows the future perfectly before it happens (Isa. 46:10) have foreseen the absentee or abandoning fathers producing families with no father? Could He have foreseen the root as to why believers today would not be able to forgive Him? Could He have possibly known that one of the greatest and most prevalent areas of unforgiveness would be children, especially sons, who would not be able to forgive their physical fathers?

The Father-hating Syndrome

We believe the answer is yes. We have seen it on our Freedom Blog on our websites, blog that was once the most visited blog of a Christian church. And even if we didn't spot it initially, women who have been married to men with the father-hating syndrome saw it. Men who have been there and been delivered saw it.

Here is the blog comment/question one man posted under a false name on a Tuesday afternoon. He asked if it was okay to keep the Sabbath by himself because he disliked the pastors. He thought it would be more peaceful. Also, would it be okay with God if he kept his family from going to church services, since he didn't want to keep the Sabbath alone.

On the blog the next day he said that he didn't like the pastors because all they did was tell him what he needed to correct in his life. He thought he was being picked on because he didn't see them correcting other people. He didn't hear any words of encouragement and love, and that is what makes people want to change.

What followed was a barrage of pot shots from women and men against the attitude of this man. The blog thread, "Enter Jesus' Day of Joy," lacked joy as invectives flew and tempers were aroused. After much blogging and praying, the truth emerged. This man hated his father and was stuck in unforgiveness to him.

It reminds one of the commercials selling drugs, which end with a litany of possible side effects such as shortness of breath, heart failure, and sudden death. The tormenting demons exposed in our book, ***God's Fruit of Forgiveness***, of which this book is a needed companion, can also bring about sudden death. And as many look to their drugs to mask the symptoms while ignoring the cause of the attacks on their health, many also prefer the fleshly solution of anger/rage, refusing to take God's solution to the mammoth problem of unforgiveness.

While a number of our perceptive bloggers, through either painful experience or prevailing prayer, pegged this man and unveiled him for who he really was, it took over two weeks before he revealed his true problem. He said that he was so glad that in the first blog he had chosen to use an alias instead of his name. He couldn't believe there were so many who hated him. He thought that he must take control of his family. As far as he was concerned, the woman had no voice in what God she served or the church she went to. Then he stated that she should have no say as to when or where she would be available to him as her husband. Her caring for the children should never ever interfere with the man's sexual needs. He saw the blog answers as twisted and evil, that it wasn't God who was giving the answers. He stated he would give the answers in his timing. He mentioned he would get even with his dad as well as the other bloggers.

The problem behind this comment was much easier to uncover than his first offerings. Anger/rage and the spirit of control were laid bare for all to see. In addition, a key element was also revealed. Sex was a god in this man's life, and he evaluated everything and everyone on what sexual satisfaction they could give him. He thought he was a good Christian, but his words and actions betrayed his real motivation. He wasn't walking the walk with Jesus. He was entangled in a complicated web of self-serving, selfishness, and self-centeredness rather than in Jesus' robe of righteousness.

Answering the Father-hater

The answers to this person came from some of our readers who have had much experience with men who display the same symptoms. They pegged him with an amazing accuracy, although some were reacting from their own bitterness and unforgiveness, stating they didn't have all the answers. His choice of words, however, plainly showed the attacks of unforgiveness, anger rage, cruelty, and control. This confirmed that the Holy Spirit was revealing to him the truth. They told him to give up his rights to get even with Jesus; vengeance belongs to Him. This way, the thirty-three demonic tormentors that are given legal right to make people miserable would no longer have control over him. They told him not to waste his breath in this hate-filled ranting and raving.

They went on to say that the comments made concerning him were not written with a perfect attitude; however, they were right on target. They showed him who he really was, not in a heartless way, but to alert him to the various personalities that had control over his loose mouth.

Another blogger wrote to him saying that they were praying that soon he would be given the grace of God to look at himself and recognize the bad attitudes that overpowered his existence. They were praying for the spirit of forgiveness and the spirit of repentance to fill him. They thanked him for having the courage to speak out in the blogs as it had opened the door to freedom to many who were or are trapped in this same condition.

They were praying he would have the freedom in Jesus, and that he and his family would be set free. They cautioned him to quit fighting God. This was one battle, strenuous and painful, that he could never win.

A teen prayer group led by a young man in a nearby town made an interesting comment, saying that he had been reading about the fake for nearly a month. The young man noted that he could see that the man was making himself unlovable, unlikeable, and ever unbearable. He told him that their prayer group was praying for his repentance in regards to his setting his will to be amoral, abnormal, and acidic as well as being addicted to his lies, his perversions, his abusiveness, and his self aggrandizement. He went on to say that five in the group had written out dreams they had the day before that were very similar. They saw a gravestone that said, "Here lies the fake." As well, ten people of the group had visions of tombstones that said, "Unforgiveness stole a fake's life." They asked for an explanation for those dreams and visions.

The dream interpretation revealed that this man had gone so far in tempting God and setting His will against Him that we needed to release him to Jesus to deal with him as only He could.

One of the comments from a Spirit-led counselor was strong. He had seen so many men in this syndrome and knew them all too well, so he gave strong medicine to this man. He wrote that he believed that this name that had been given him as the "fake" suited him. He told him that his ravings were red herrings to get control of others and they would soon backfire. His choice to make himself blind to his unforgiveness, bitterness, perversions, lying, deceitful practices, and even the words of mockery were a cesspool of conceit and pride that would soon suck him under. That cesspool usually leads to death, suicide, or jail. He basically said, "take your pick!" He personally thought this man needed a woman like Maureen McT, confident enough to "beat the snot" out of him whenever she thought he needed it. "Rest in peace," he finished.

As you can see, we had a lively blog. Our bloggers pulled no punches when they spotted a phony, someone trying to cover up serious issues. Many of them were dedicated and gifted prayer warriors. You can read in the Introduction to this book the prayers of one of them and the results those all-night prayers brought.

Another turnaround that resulted was expressed by another blogger. Many people had advised him to check out the blogs on this site. He was so glad that he did. He saw that he was heading in the very same direction as this other guy, the fake. He had slipped into unforgiveness without realizing it. His stepfather had sexually abused him for nearly five years before he was able to get out of the house. He had been rehearsing the pain, reliving it every night, totally incapable of keeping a friendship or a relationship. He was going insane with his lust for vengeance.

He knew that someone close to him was praying, and he kept asking God to release him from his stepfather and what had been done to him. Hope against hope kept him going as he waited to be free. As soon as he read the other men's experiences, he knew he had to declare out loud that he forgave his stepfather for every vile thing he had done to him. He then had peace in his heart and desired to be clean in Jesus. He thanked everyone who spoke out prayers in the Spirit and declared God's blessing on them all.

Why the End-time Plague of Unforgiveness?

Why are so many Christians in unforgiveness? The answer is manifold. One reason is that words in Job, words by Job himself and by Satan, prophesied Satan's power over believers in the last days.

In Job 2:5, Satan taunted, "However, put forth Your hand now, and touch his bone and his flesh; he will curse You to Your face."

This verse prophesied that Christians (as well as others) would curse God because of the fear of loss in their lives in the time of tribulation that is upon us now. Job was attacked, but he didn't let the fear of loss get the best of him. He stood fast in his integrity and refused to curse God. But Satan's words revealed his end-time plan and spoke a prophecy that would be fulfilled. In the economic crises that affect even Christians, many of them have cursed God because of what He has allowed in their lives. They haven't forgiven Him.

Jesus responded to Satan, "Behold, he is in your power, only spare his life" (Job 2:6). It seems in this time of tribulation that Christians are under Satan's power. They have allowed him to have influence in their lives as he comes down with greater wrath because his time has been cut short (Rev. 12:12). His own words and actions against believers have caused him to shorten his time to rule on the earth, and he knows it.

Nevertheless, Christians continue to fall for his ruses, as Satan himself predicted in Job. And one of his major traps in this end time is in the area of forgiveness. He has spread the prevalent lie that forgiveness is wrong, a sign of weakness, and that you need to stand up and exercise your right to get back at the person who hurt you. Many Christians feel justified in their refusal to forgive, expecting the offenders to come humbly before them and ask for forgiveness or it will not be extended.

They forget that God gave them unconditional forgiveness before they were even created, as we explained to a questioner on our blog. He was asking who doesn't forgive his father for something? He figured he had a very good reason to kill his father rather than forgive him. He didn't understand, however, how such an attitude was related to the drug addiction problem he was trying to break.

Our answer cited that his words clearly showed that he hadn't forgiven his dad, so God couldn't forgive him until he sought the grace of God to forgive. At this point God couldn't even hear his prayers (Isa. 59:1-3). Only through his forgiveness of his stepfather could he be released from the addiction. This is something he couldn't overcome by himself, and if God's not hearing him, no help could come. The first step is to realize that even though he has good reason, so he thinks, to kill his dad, so did God have good reason to kill him for all the sins he has committed, but God, the Father sent Jesus to die for him. He chose to allow him to be forgiven even though He could wipe him from the face of the earth.

He was also given a prayer to speak out from an inspired blogger that will help him…

This blogger led him to acknowledge and confess by saying out loud, "Father, I need Jesus; I have made a mess out of my life. I have made wrong choices, errors in judgment and walked in prideful sin. I ask for your knowledge, wisdom, and understanding to know how to walk with Jesus and know the truth of Your Word. I turn my will over to you. Teach me and adjust wherever you see something that needs adjusting. I ask for the spirit of forgiveness, repentance, and love.

Thank You for this fresh start and every bit of strength that I need to make the changes necessary to walk like Jesus. In Jesus' Name, amen." The inspired blogger also encouraged him to start reading the Bible. Do you?

CHAPTER 5

Our Father's Love for Us

In these last days the heart of the Father Love is turning to His children. The problem is this: most Christians haven't received a heart revelation of that love.

A famous Christian, Whitney Houston, sang as she often did, a short time before she died, that well-known song, "Jesus loves me, this I know, for the Bible tells me so…"

Many Christians don't read the Bible. And if they do, they don't read the first part. Furthermore, they don't read it aloud so that the words go into their hearts. Their hearts are not assured from the Word of God that our Father really loves them.

Satan has so attacked Christians, most often because they have been deprived of the knowledge of the truth, with so many problems that Christians wonder if God truly loves them. "Why would I have these tragic events in my life if God loves me?" "Why, why, why?" "Why am I not blessed?" These are the questions they ask.

That's because they aren't sure from the Word of God and from what God has already given them that our Father loves them.

God assures us that His sheep hear His voice. It was when I began to hear God tell me Himself that He loved and appreciated me that I finally realized in my heart that my Father truly loved me. I had to hear it directly from Him.

Christians are often falsely taught that they must somehow earn God's love. They must do something in order to be loved by Him. They must repent or God won't show His kindness to them.

It's the other way around. God says that His kindness and goodness leads us to change our ways to be like Him (Rom. 2:4). Jesus told the woman caught in the act of adultery, "I don't condemn you. Go and sin no more." He told the five-time divorcee who was living with another guy at the time, "I want to give you living water to drink."

Christians often believe the opposite: "Go and sin no more, and then I won't condemn you. I'll love you when you get your act together." This isn't biblical. This isn't God. This isn't love—or rather Love, since that's God's name (1 John 4:8).

We need a biblical and heart revelation of the Father's love for us. When we receive it, it will transform our thoughts and our lives. We will gain a newfound reverential awe of our Father and His love that will lead us to change our lives, to stand in awe of all of God's instructions for us so that we obey Him and receive all His blessings, not just the crumbs that fall from the Master's table.

Are you receiving only crumbs rather than the fullness of God's covenant blessings? Or are you a true believer who has received in Jesus the full revelation of the Father's love for you?

His Own Didn't Receive Him

John 1:11-12 tells us that Jesus, who came to reveal the Father and His love, came to His own, who did not receive Him. John is not simply talking about the Jews, but about His own people, Christians, who have not received Jesus and the right to become children and sons of God and "believe in His name."

John later in His epistles speaks of believers whose hearts condemns them and steals their confidence of being loved by the Father. They don't do what is pleasing in God's sight because they don't have their identity set in Jesus as being loved by the Father as Jesus is. They don't obey His commandments.

John explains, "This is His commandment, that we believe in the *name* of His Son Jesus Christ, and love one another, just as He commanded us" (1 John 3:23).

John said the same thing in John 1:12, that those who truly receive Jesus and thus have the door opened to know the Father and His love, "believe in His name."

The two key factors in the end-time children of God turning to the Father by knowing Jesus, the Door to the Father, are overlooked as details by the church today.   In our other books we have written volumes on these two points, the litmus test for true believers in the last days, the two gut checks, if you will, that will separate those who turn to the Father's heart and those who don't.

I'm talking about meeting Jesus on His day, the day most Christians think is somehow Jewish and outdated, part of a "law" they think is good except for this one point that bugs them. Yes, I'm talking about that seventh-day Sabbath, the *only* Sabbath Jesus told us to remember, the one we have chosen to forget. When we meet Him at the appointed time, we gain special intimacy with Him and the Father, allowing us to connect to the Father's heart of love on His day of love.

Fellow South Carolinian Shane Willard, pastor and evangelist, has been accused of making God out to be too kind. Nevertheless, this man of God, mentored by a rabbi in understanding how Hebrews understand the Bible, speaks truth in a fresh, exciting way—truth that brings great understanding of the Father's love. I learned some of the concepts in this chapter from Shane, and I thank him for relating the knowledge he gleaned from his rabbi friend.

With the aid of his unique and humorous teaching gift, he explains just how good and awesome a God we have. He does it through the depth of understanding of Hebrew words and culture.

The revelation he gives will bring more understanding if you grasp the second end-time gut check: the name of Jesus. His name alone brings salvation (Acts 4:12) as well as intimacy, anointing, healing, and power. A title such as Lord doesn't bring those blessings, yet many Christians today almost exclusively refer to Jesus as Lord without mentioning His name, Jesus.

Notice how "the apostle whom Jesus loved" emphasizes in the passages cited the importance of believing in and on the name of Jesus. That's only one of the reasons John knew in his heart He was loved. He called Jesus by name. He knew him intimately, not in a gay way, but in a profound way.

The Doorway of Jesus and His Name

Jesus came to reveal the Father, and He said that if we saw and knew Him, we would know the Father. John knew Jesus, so he also began to know and receive the Father's love as He received Jesus' love. If Lord or the Lord is your doorway to the Father, perhaps you should find a better door, Jesus. Our church has been transformed since we received this revelation about the name of Jesus early in our ministry. We have seen the truth of the power of His name by the fruits.

We understand that the entire Christian world uses the term Lord, and God knows why and meets believers where they are in His mercy. He wants to reveal the importance of the name of Jesus in these last days, and we are blessed to begin to open this blessing in small way to those who read. We thank God that this wonderful truth will be revealed to the body of Jesus so the bride can be intimate with the Bridegroom and be ready to meet Him. We thank God it will be done in His timing and with love and mercy.

If you think you have intimacy and power now as you use "Lord" more often than Jesus, think of where you would be by using His name exclusively. Try it and see if you have the same experience we did.

I hope these two revelations, which take great courage to practice, since you will be going against the mainstream, will allow you to begin to discover how great the Father's love is for you. And I hope in sharing insights from both the pictorial Hebrew and the conceptual Hebrew that you will see the Bible and God's love in a new light.

My greatest desire is to see the revelation of the Father's love begin to be a heart experience for all of us. We don't need to wonder if our Father loves us anymore. The Bible tells us so. But maybe you haven't understood just how powerful this statement of God's love is in the original language. Stay tuned.

The Bible prophesies that in these last days those who have "a form of godliness" (Christians, 2 Tim. 3:1-6) would be lovers of pleasure and money rather than lovers of God.

Once again, I'll let the apostle of love explain this: he tells us not to love the world and worldly ways. He also tells us the problem with Christians who love the world and its lusts more than God: "the love of the Father is not in him" (1 John 2:15). He doesn't love the Father by obeying Him because he has not internalized in his heart the important truth that the Father loves *him*.

When he realizes how good and loving the Father is towards *him*, he then begins to respond to that love with a profound desire to avoid displeasing His Father in any way. That is often the way we describe our "first love," that exuberant, zealous desire to please God by keeping every detail of His Word and being hungry to learn that Word.

Some of us are Ephesians at heart, or like the members of the church of Ephesus and the Ephesus or first church era. We have lost that first love. Others have lost it so much they have become nonchalant, neither cold nor hot, and that is the general condition of the whole church now in the present Laodicean era (Rev.3:14).

The remnant who truly "receive" Jesus (John 1:11) by meeting Him on His day and calling out His name, Jesus, will recapture their first love for the Father born of their realization of His love for them. They will repent, and those with a lukewarm condition will repent of their lackadaisical attitude. They will be raptured to enjoy the love of the Father in a special, intimate, firsthand way.

We need to understand an important principle we may have overlooked as we seek to know God loves us "for the Bible tells us so." What does the Bible tell us indeed?

The Bible Shows Us Our Father Loves Us

Peter tells us that if we address God as Father, we are called to walk in reverent awe and obedience to Him (1 Pet. 1:17-18). That proper fear of our Father, which is more akin to a reverence based in love, is rooted and grounded in the truth that our Father had already sacrificed Jesus before the foundation of the world (1 Pet. 1:19-20).

The apostle of love, John, also assured us of this love. He shows us that the Father wrote us into the book of life and that Jesus was slain from the foundation of the world (Rev. 13:8). This is a strong indication that Jesus, the Word, looked to the One we call Father as His Father before He was born of a virgin. He has been intimate, truly One, with His Father from before time began, and that was His prayer for us in John 17:22-26.

Our Father knows the end from the beginning. He foreknew and foreknows every single wretched sin we will ever commit in our lifetimes. And knowing every sin we have or will commit, He still forgave us before we committed these sins, and He planned every detail of giving up His only Son at that time so He could shower all His love on us as He did and does on Jesus. Now that's love! That's the essence of the Father's love.

We don't have to earn anything. We don't need to feel we need to earn our Father's love. He already for all intents and purposes sacrificed His only Son for us so He could have us in His Family of Love, all the while knowing our worst sins. He knew it all, and yet He gave up His Son so Jesus could have many brothers and sisters and our Father could have an expanding family of precious sons and daughters who would always know they are loved.

What comes across as we read the writings of the New Testament is that the writers speak of God's promises as a done deal. Everything was done before the foundation of the world. It had to be finalized, of course, when Jesus went to the cross and said, "It is finished." His resurrection and ascension sealed the deal, the blood covenant we have with our Father in Jesus.

It's a Done Deal!

The writer of Hebrews makes an amazing statement. He says that God swore in His wrath that Israel wouldn't enter His rest "although His works were finished from the foundation of the world" (Heb. 4:3). While the next verse situates the context by saying that Jesus rested from His work of "recreation" on the first seventh-day Sabbath, the other passages we have cited make it clear the writer is explaining a concept: God's works were finished well before the foundation of the earth, estimated to be about four billion years ago.

Everything God does for us, He has already done. All we need to do is accept it in faith and thank Him for it. That's all. We don't have to do penance and beat ourselves up until God is pleased with us.

Jesus died for us in God's way of thinking (which should be ours!) before the worlds or we were actually created. And God gives us all things in Jesus. Salvation. Healing. Prosperity. Protection. Provision. Rest in Jesus.

How do we know this? How can we be sure God loves us? It's all recorded in Genesis 1:1. You could write an encyclopedia to fully explain that verse. Even considering the Hebrew pictures in letters and words, it says a lot. Each Hebrew letter is a picture, and each word is akin to a comic strip, if you will. It's a picture language, and when we understand the first few verses of Genesis 1 we begin to get the picture of how much God loves us.

Are you ready to get the picture? Here is the transliteration into English letters of the first verse, consisting of seven verses, of which the middle verse in Hebrew thought is the main point. So what is the main point of this verse? It reads: *Bereishit bara Elohim* **et** *hashamayim ve'***et** *ha'aretz*. The transliteration of *aleph-tav* is rendered *et* here (see the unitalicized word in bold), whereas *aleph* is equivalent to our *a*.

That central word is a grammatical construction that is isn't translated. It's used seven thousand times in the Hebrew Scriptures. Some scholars have puzzled as to why. There is more to this grammatical word than meets most eyes, as confirmed by a rabbi I interviewed recently.

The word is *aleph-tav.* That's the Hebrew equivalent of a name we know well. It's the *Alpha-Omega* as revealed in Revelation. Interesting, isn't it? It's Jesus in the first verse of the Bible! The beginning of the Bible and the end come together. In the last chapter (Rev. 22:13) and first chapter of the Bible, it's the name above all names that is the focus. The Kingdom of God is the main message Jesus gave, and the Bible is the truth of the Kingdom and the King, Jesus. He is the beginning and the end, and He is in the first chapter and the last. Look for the *et* in the middle.

What is even more interesting is that the *aleph-tav* appears in the sixth word as well. He came as the God of the First Testament, the Word who spoke to man, and He came a second time as a man born of a woman to reveal the Father who was not known in the Hebrew Scriptures.

Cross Prophesied in Genesis

However, that's not all. A letter precedes the last *aleph-tav.* It's *vav,* the letter whose picture meaning is the nail. He came a second time to be nailed to a cross to redeem us. In God's mind it was already done before the world began. God had everything taken care of before He created the earth. He foreknew every detail of everything that would happen. After all, He is God, and that foreknowledge is one of the things that make Him God.

God foreknew that Satan would corrupt the perfect universe He created from nothing, and that Adam would allow the devil to pervert even the perfect Eden He created on a reformed earth.

Then the earth became *tohu va bohu.* This word *tohu* means "incapable of distinguishing real from not real," or crazy. The earth that Satan corrupted and later perverted through Adam became crazy and in need of redemption. If you take the meaning of the letters, it means that the earth became crazy because of a lack of revelation of the covenant of the nail, Jesus' sacrifice on the cross.

The first letter of *bohu* signifies house and means the house God made on earth became uninhabitable because of the craziness Satan introduced. That's because the house didn't have a revelation of the covenant of the nail revealed in verse 1.

The word for darkness, *chosheq,* signifies that the boundaries you chose consume your covering. The words indicate that this pattern of disrepair was presenting itself in the face of God's hidden blessings. The Holy Spirit hovered over the deep. This word for hovered can mean to grow soft or relax. *Mayim* or waters also means chaos or open-handed violence, so God relaxed in the face of this slap in the face, and as Jesus said to do later, turned the cheek to this rebellion.

Jesus said, "Light be." This not only means that light could now be seen but that the Light of the world, Jesus, would bring light into the world's darkness in every way, as John 1 explains. The One who is Light would shine.

Light is *orah*, and when you put the *tav* before it, it becomes *torah,* which also signifies, "that which comes from the man nailed to the cross." Jesus was both the *orah* and the *Torah*.

God outsmarted the rebellion of Satan and man by preparing and speaking into being the sacrifice of Jesus before the world began. The darkness of Satan is never a match for the Light that is Jesus. And when we let Him shine through us, Satan hasn't got a prayer.

God intimated that Satan would do his work after God did his. God repeated the truth that *He* had finished *His* works that *He* had made, implying that Satan would do *his* work to defeat God's plan.

In fact, Genesis 2:3 is a powerful declaration to God's people and to all life forms in the universe that His Sabbath covenant would protect those who keep it from any of the many hosts of heaven should they attack His people in the last days. Jesus will "punish the host of heaven on high" (Isa. 24:21) at the very end.

No protection will exist apart from the Sabbath covenant. Those who don't keep God's days will have no defense against the aliens, giants, and other life forms in the galaxies that will attack in the last days. For those who dwell in the light of the Father's presence and rest on His secure lap on His day, no darkness can defeat them.

God tells us not to love the world of darkness but to love the Light. "If anyone loves the world, the love of the Father is not in him" (1 John 2:15). He doesn't have the *agape* love of Father God in him because he hasn't received the revelation of Genesis 1:1, that the Father has proved His love to him before the world began, doing everything for him while foreknowing all of his failures. Because he hasn't had a revelation of the Father's love for him, He hasn't begun to stand in awe of His Father, turning his heart toward Him by respecting and obeying Him. Without that respect, he can't have value and can't realize his value and live accordingly, valuing others as he values himself.

Restoring the Respect of the Father

The New International translation of Isaiah 33:5-6 explains this concept. Our Father has filled Zion or the church with justice and righteousness by sending us Jesus. Our God is a "wealth of salvation, wisdom and knowledge; the fear [or reverent obedience] of the Father is the key to this treasure."

The Father draws us to Jesus, and in Him we begin to realize how much our Father loves us by giving us His Son. This allows us to begin to stand in awe of our Father's awesome power and keep from disobeying Him at all costs. That's our first love and respectful obedience of our Father that many Christians have lost or never had.

That is what must be restored in this end time. A work of Elijah was to restore all things, and that includes the turning of the heart of God's children back to Him in love and reverent obedience.

Young's Literal Translation shows the importance of the reverential obedience of our heavenly Father: "The end of the whole matter let us hear: Fear God, and keep His commands, for this [is] the whole of man" (Eccl. 12:13). This is the conclusion the wisest man who ever lived before Jesus, Solomon, came to after the best life and then the worst life a man can have. He married foreign women and went after their gods, abandoning God in a backslidden condition like no other.

He committed every sin he could possibly commit and experienced every sexual deviation he could have, but his emptiness brought him back to the respectful obedience he had once exemplified.

The reverential respect and obedience of the Father God, Solomon said, is the "whole of man." Without it, wholeness or value is impossible. You can't understand your value in God's and your eyes without a profound respect of the Father and His commandments, which were the same that Jesus gave in both testaments. You can only value and love others as you value and love yourself. Without respect for the Father, you don't realize your value.

The first phrase in Jesus' model prayer for us is "Our Father who is in heaven, hallowed be Your name." His name is to be held in the highest respect. That is the beginning of the recommended prayer Jesus gave, and it is the beginning of a life of value to self and others.

The reverence of the Father is "the beginning of knowledge" (Prov. 1:7). The father/son dialogue in Proverbs 2:1-6 is a conversation our heavenly Father could have with us: "If you will receive My words and treasure My commandments, then you will discern the proper reverential respect for and obedience to Me, your Father."

That paraphrased promise is the beginning of knowledge and wisdom. It is the essence of the whole man, the man who recognizes his value in God's sight.

When we realize that our Father has already done everything for us as revealed in Hebrews 4 and Genesis 1, we can indeed respond to Him in the awe and obedience He deserves, and in so doing we will realize in Jesus how worthy and valuable we are, and then we can show love and respect to others and shine God's light in this world.

We are called to preach the gospel of the Kingdom of God, the Kingdom of Love, in this world, and the end of the age will come. We need to internalize our Father's Love for us if we are to preach this Kingdom of Love with our voices and above all, with the good examples we set.

Our anointing is to help those who in Isaiah 58 say, "Why have we fasted and You do not see? Why have we humbled ourselves and You do not notice?" (Isa. 58:3). "Why don't you love us, Father?" is what they are saying. "Why don't you protect us? Why do you allow us to experience the results of our words and actions?" Our calling is to pray and fast for them to see them set free, and to give them the good news of the Kingdom of Love because we have personally experienced that love from our Father.

Frenzied Values That Keep Us from Seeing Ourselves as Sons

Satan is moving to wear down the saints (Dan. 7:25) so they can't see themselves as sons of our Father Love. Believers are losing the battle by insisting on praising Satan for his attacks, pains, losses, and inconveniences. Satan is trying to overpower believers (Dan. 7:21). But why is what Satan is doing now so much more important than what Jesus has already done for us?

The answer is that we live in a frenzied, fast-paced world in which we establish different criteria for values other than our Father's. Following are some of these values, some of the things we say:

- I'm strong. I can do it myself.
- I'm smart. I can think things out myself.
- I'm a good provider. I can provide for my family.
- I'm here to defend my family. No one can do it better.
- I'm the best. I earn my own promotions.
- I work for a living. I don't rely on others.
- I don't have to tell my family that I love them. They just know it.
- Everyone knows I'm the best, because they come to me for help.

These sets of values are the backbone for failures, burnout, and mental breakdowns. They also open the door for procrastination, sloth, and the desire to speak out the words of death. Addictions of all kinds come because of this route of frenzied values, and because they haven't been turned over to Jesus.

The root of these frenzied values is an important theme of this book: not accepting that our Father loves us. The following situations set us up to be the victims of these frenzied values. These are items to turn over to Jesus on the new moon. We can call these the cornerstones for the frenzied life:

- Being treated as collateral as a child. You are owned, not loved.
- Not being told that you are loved and appreciated.
- Being condemned, ostracized, and silenced by parents. They had no time to listen.
- Seeing oneself as nothing but a workhorse.
- Having your ideas and concepts shot down without discussion or further input.
- Being devalued by being yelled at, screamed at, cursed at, and labeled.
- Not being taught morals, judgments, and values according to the Word of God, but taught only by tradition.
- Having perfection demanded of you before you are taught precepts and requirements of the job that needs to be learned or done.
- Being compared to others who have different talents, backgrounds, motivations, and anointings.
- Not being told that you are forgiven for any and all shortcomings, sins, breakages, failures, and past mistakes. You are given no second chance.

These cornerstones are the groundwork for not putting our trust in Jesus, not believing that our Father loves us, and not accepting that we are called to be sons of God.

When these cornerstones are firmly laid, Satan attacks with multiple levels of fear, bringing fear of correction, fear of discipline, and the sound of the Word of God.

Both Joseph and Abraham learned to reject frenzied values and find success. You can too, if you lay down these false cornerstones and frenzied values to Jesus on the new moon.

The whole world is as if on tiptoes, waiting for the revelation and maturing of the sons of God, waiting on believers in these last days to realize how much their Father has turned His heart of love toward them from time immemorial, and then to turn their hearts in love, awe, respect, and obedience to their Father Love.

The earth doesn't have to be cursed. We, the sons and daughters of our Father, can come to the fore and demonstrate the value our Father has given us, shining His light in this dark world. Will we prevent the destruction of this planet? Will we be the force that preserves the earth and allows Jesus to return in glory to transform this earth into a Garden of Eden? We have been given that great challenge. We shall rise to meet it!

CHAPTER 6

In Trials, We Ask, "Where Did Your Love Go?"

The pressure is on. Jesus said that in the world we would have tribulation (John 16:33), and we are now in the midst of *the* end-time tribulation. Job laid the foundation for all last days' prophecies, and his words and actions prophesied severe trials for the believers.

Because of these trials that God has allowed and that are necessary for the purification of the Bride of Jesus in these last days, many Christians have become discouraged, wondering if their Father in heaven really loves them. Trials can make us or break us, and for some, difficult times have kept them from turning their hearts back to Father Love.

The Supremes sang a song years ago entitled, "Where Did Our Love Go?" It's a song of sadness and desperation of a woman who believes her beau doesn't love her anymore. And we sometimes are attacked with the same feeling in regards to the Bridegroom of the church, Jesus, and in regards to our relationship with our Father in heaven. We sometimes ask of Him, "Where did Your love go?"

Job never cursed God, and he knew He was loved. Nevertheless, he had moments where he wondered what was going on in his life and what God was doing. We can only grasp the powerful portent of Job's words by understanding the multifaceted and conceptual meaning of those words. In several places he prophesied a time of darkness and trials upon Jesus and His end-time followers, a time when they would be tempted to question the Father's love.

Conceptual languages are hard to translate. They contain many meanings, even positive and negative meanings, in one word. No linear language like English can possibly render the full meaning of the words of the conceptual, vast meaning of the original Hebrew. My friend and apostolic leader Gerald Budzinski asked God years ago for supernatural help to understand the conceptual Hebrew, and a prominent Canadian rabbi has confirmed that his prayers were answered. I share in this chapter some of the revelations that we are able to grasp.

Job 3:10 is such a conceptual prophecy, as properly translated from the Hebrew: "Therefore, inasmuch as darkness could not hide the truth nor the Word and prophecies of God to bring in ignorance, nor could darkness close off or shut out the heart of my soul, and even though darkness has bound me to see all its misery, perverseness, and iniquity that it has schemed in the years of sorrow and tribulation, with my inner eyes my soul sees it."

Job was prophesying a time when darkness tries to hide the existence of the real Jesus, as in the Dark Ages and in these last dark days. He foretold darkness for Jesus, attacking him at His birth and as a young child, darkness that would try to steal His anointing, peace, and joy, and that would try to incite Him to anger and ultimately kill Him. The same attacks come against His followers, especially in the last days.

Jesus amplified Job's prophecies by saying a time of lawlessness and betrayal would extinguish the love of many, even believers (Mat. 24:10-13). Only those who would know the love of their Father and persevere in their love for Him would endure to the end.

Job asked why. So do we. His whys prophesied what we would go through in these last days. His questions are our questions. We have similar pressures and sometimes feel like giving up. He also prophesied that some of us wouldn't give up.

"Why Must I Go Through This Mess?"

The questions that Job asked as he wondered what God was doing in his life would be questions that we would all have to face in these last days. While the English translations of Job 3:11-12 veil the full meaning, he was asking questions that many Christians asked today: " Why did God not take me to heaven when I was baptized? Why did I have to see and go through all this mess? Why has life become so hard for me? Why have the pressures of sin been stronger against me after accepting Jesus than before? Why is my flesh warring against my spirit so much that I long for death? Why are Satan and the pressures of the world oppressing me and blocking my success?"

Job was a king who had lost his status and prosperity, as well as his family. He was asking God, "Why didn't I die when I was taken from the chariot of power, wealth, and family? Why am I dumped into dust and ashes when I am doing everything You asked of me?"

As Job, we believers are called righteous and made righteous by accepting Jesus as Savior, Master, Redeemer, and God. We have submitted to baptism, going into the womb of death to be reborn into the light of life in Jesus.

Job faced three times fiery trials by Satan. At each level of overcoming, we appear to backslide three times in the process of overcoming the flesh, the world, and Satan. We continue our backsliding into darkness until we realize our total dependence on Jesus for His blood, His strength, His wisdom, and His coat of righteousness.

In all his trials, unknown to Job, Jesus had told Satan not to take his life. In the same way, while we pass through the valley of the shadow of death, God has promised us that we won't die in these trials unless we submit to Satan.

Our Father's Love Never Fails

Job asked In Job 3:12, "Why did the knees receive me, and why the breasts, that I should suck?" When we consider the Hebrew, Job was asking, "Why was I blessed and protected until this attack? Where did Your love go, God, when things started going bad in my life? I saw Your love in the good times, but where is it in all these attacks? Where now is the comfort and provision of the abundant Provider *El Shaddai*?"

Jesus had to answer those questions on the way to the cross, and each of us in these last days must answer those questions.

"Does God still love me in times of trial? Does my Father Love truly care about what's happening to me?" These are the questions we must answer as we seek to turn our hearts to our Father.

Will the loss of something or even everything cause us to lose our love, understanding, and loyalty to Jesus? Would the loss of a pastor, apostle, teacher, mate, or child cause us to leave the church of God and the love of Jesus?

Many of us have asked Job's questions: "Why did You let me taste of Your goodness and then see it all taken away? Why did my mate and children seem to come to Jesus and then flee? Why was I healthy and then attacked with sickness?" David asked the same kind of questions in the Psalms.

Job was saying to God, "I didn't ask to be a king, to be special, to get any special treatment. So why am I being singled out to be tried like this?"

We are also called to be kings. And the reason we are called is the reason Job was called: God knew that in our weakness we would humbly seek His help and rely on Him for correction and guidance.

Jesus and Job both prophesied that problems would come our way. Persecutions and demonic forces would try to break us of our resolve. Yet Jesus said, "… take courage; I have overcome the world" (John 16:33).

Moreover, He told us not to worry (Mat. 6:25; Phil. 4:6) and to go about the mission He gave us in Matthew 28:19-20, where He said, "I am with you always, even to the end of the age."

He and Job were prophesying great troubles for us in the last days, but Job's steadfastness in trial and Jesus' words to us tell us that our Savior and Defender will never abandon us and will especially be with us in these last days.

The words of Job and his prophecies have been overlooked because of the false doctrine that the Old Testament, as men call it, is done away. Nothing could be further from the truth.

Here are God's words of encouragement to us believers today, as we face the most turbulent and yet most exciting times in history: "For whatever was written in earlier times was written for our instruction, so that through perseverance and the encouragement of the Scriptures we might have hope. Now may the God who gives perseverance and encouragement grant you to be of the same mind with one another according to Christ Jesus" (Romans 15:4).

Jesus has declared that we are His witnesses and that no one, no person or demon, can snatch us out of His hand of love (Isa. 43:11-13; John 10:28-29). Our Father promises us that He will finish the work He started in us (Phil 1:6) and will be faithful to present us blameless before Jesus as His bride (1 Thes. 5:23-24). He encourages us not to lose heart and allow the trials to weary us (Gal. 6:9). Job didn't have all the answers, but because of Job's experience and Jesus' words, we do have access to the answers.

Satan may cause events that make it seem like God has let go of us. He hasn't. So let's not let go of Jesus. Let's turn our hearts to our Father, who is Love, and whose love for us never fails.

We mustn't let the pressures from Satan and the world break us. They should *make* us. God's Word gives us the encouragement we need to turn our hearts to our Father Love and know in our hearts that He loves us: "Now may the God of hope fill you with all joy and peace in believing, so that you will abound in hope by the power of the Holy Spirit" (Romans 15:13).

Where did God's love go? It never went anywhere. Our Father's love has been with us through all the tough times, and as we turn our hearts to Him, He will lead us through the valleys of these last days, and we will dwell in His house of love forever. Sometimes our only solution is to hold onto Jesus' hand and trust Him to lead us, not away from, but *through* the valley of the shadow of death. In the days of heavy persecution of believers and the attacks of ISIS, never before have true believers needed to trust their Shepherd.

Satan's Attacks

Satan will try everything up his sleeve to get us to believe God doesn't love us, throwing trials at us that God allows for a purpose. Remember, however, that as the devil accuses us "before our God day and night"(Rev. 12:11), our High Priest Jesus counters his attacks day and night as well (Heb. 7:25).

Satan knows that if he can get us to condemn ourselves, we cannot receive all the gifts God wants to pour out upon us (1 John 3:21-22). We must understand that condemning ourselves is a slippery slope leading to the demonic world. It is worse than the sin committed that makes us feel guilty. Both sin and guilt must be turned over to Jesus.

That's what John is telling us in the above verses. He's giving us the conditions for receiving the blessings of the Father of lights who loves to shower gifts on His children (James 1:17). We must know how much our Father loves us so we can come boldly before Him with absolute confidence in our identity in Jesus and in God's covenant promises, keeping His commandments and doing what is pleasing in His sight.

Few realize what Job released in his conceptual Hebrew prophecies. Job probably didn't either. But they opened up the concept that the Israelites couldn't grasp: ask in faith and confidence, and you shall receive all the gifts God has to give. Jesus told us to ask, seek, and knock on His door for anything we wanted (Mat. 7:7-8), and the rest of the Bible shows those actions should always be framed in thanksgiving, not doubt.

Finding the Woman of Your Dreams
Just a Walk in the Park

Here's an example of the power of thanks, found in a comment by a young man on our blog. He had been thanking our Father for bringing the woman that He wanted him to marry into his life. Lo and behold, while walking in the park one day, he met the woman of his dreams. He would never have thought that he would meet someone in a park.

She is a strong believer in Jesus and even keeps the Sabbath. And they both know that God introduced them.

Our response underlines the power of thanksgiving: "Thank you for that powerful testimony of the power of thanksgiving. God does meet us where we are, yet when we are in thanksgiving and see our demand on His covenant as done, He meets us more quickly with the manifestation of our request. He says, 'Oh that My people would listen to Me, that [the believers] would walk in My ways! I would quickly subdue their enemies...I would feed you with the finest of the wheat, and with honey from the rock I would satisfy you' (Ps. 81:13-14,16). See how quickly you received your "honey"! Yes, God meets various people in various ways to find their mates, but this way you mentioned is a powerful one, based in thanksgiving. Wow! Nothing indeed is impossible with God. He turned [one man] around in twelve hours, and raised [a girl] from the dead after ten minutes being asleep and declared dead by doctors. But what do they know compared to our God? Thank you all for your praise reports as we glorify our great God together!"

Our Father is ready to pour out the blessings (Luke 11:13; James 1:17). Asking is a form of demand, a demand we place on the covenants we have with God. Job used a Hebrew word (*zakar*) in Job 10:9 to say to God, "Remember *now* my covenant with you." He was bold in calling for action according to the covenants. It's a law in heaven and earth: we have a right to claim our covenants.

James follows through on Job's prophecies for the last days, and we shall use paraphrases that amplify the meaning: "But if any of you lacks wisdom, have him ask of God, who gives to all men generously and without reproach or condemnation, and it will be given to him. But have him ask in faith without doubting, for the one who doubts is like the surf of the sea, driven and tossed by the wind" (James 1:5-6).

Stay Steadfast and Count Trials as Joy

Satan will try to blow us over with his winds and drown us with his floods, but James tells us what our answer should be: "Consider it all joy, my brethren, when you encounter various trials, knowing that these trials are tests of your faith that produce endurance, steadfastness, and maturity, and they allow endurance to work its maturing result, that you may be perfect and complete, lacking in nothing" (James 1:2-4).

Satan wants us double minded and insecure in our knowledge of who God really is and what He is doing in our lives. While Job was not always steadfast in joy, he never cursed God or showed unforgiveness to his tormenting friends or to those who stole his wealth. The questions he asked weren't posed out of pride or self-righteousness. He truly wanted to understand what was going on and dared to ask God openly about the situation.

His words and his steadfastness opened the door for us to succeed in these end times. These trials of the last days are testing our faith and trust in God to bring us to steadfastness and maturity in Jesus. We can rejoice because these trials are testing us for our preparedness to receive everything God has for us.

James then presents a new set of warnings I paraphrase: "For allow not that double minded man to expect that he will receive from the Divine Master, for a double minded man is fighting God and is unstable in all his ways. But the steadfast brother is glorified in his teachability and growth to full maturity. And he who is rich in double mindedness is humiliated because like the flower of grass that dies in the day, he too will pass away" (James 1:7-10).

The faith/doubt circle is a road to dizziness and confusion. Many Christians who concentrate on Lord worship rather than Jesus worship don't know they are calling on a demon who calls himself Lord, but whose name is quagmire. He majors in pushing a person from one ditch to the other, as an errant boat is pushed one way and the other by the winds.

James tells us to be teachable in our trials so that we may be glorified in our growth and maturity rather than surrendering our gifts to Satan by our divided loyalties. Our joy in Jesus will get us through all such trials. We reach our hand out to Jesus to lead us safely through the valley of the shadow of death. Our endurance will produce growth in faith, hope, and love. We will thus call for everything we have asked for to come to us as a loving gift from our Father.

"Blessed is the man who perseveres, endures, and is steadfast under trial; for once he has been approved, he will receive the crown of life, which Jesus has promised to those who love Him" (James 1:12). Because Job stood steadfast, his words opened the door for us to do the same. And because Jesus broke Satan's hold that Job had authorized, we have the crown of life and our names written in the book of life.

Stay in the joy of Jesus. Keep on obeying and loving Him even in tough times. Ask for the strength to endure in Jesus all tests, trials, and temptations. The gifts are yours when you ask without doubting.

God tests us at times, but he never tempts us (James 1:13-14). Job was attacked with doubt because it looked like God was tempting him to sin to compromise his integrity. His doubts prophesied that we would also be attacked with doubt in these last days, but his steadfastness opened the door for us to conquer our lusts. We ask amiss when we allow our lusts to take over. By dwelling on our lusts, we open the door to all sin.

Glorious Freedom from "Pet Sins"

Some things we dwell on become "pet sins." They are usually besetting weaknesses we think will make us righteous when we overcome them. We're already righteous in Jesus, but we hang onto these sins and habits and often love them more than Jesus. They are usually the last lusts to go by God's grace, since in most cases God has to build up to a certain level of faith before we are willing to let them go.

We may lay them down to Jesus repeatedly, but we take them up again until our will is fixed to say no to these sins. We turn many problems over to Jesus before we're finally willing to turn these persistent weaknesses over to Him for good.

Mark Detrick confessed on cbn.com his thirty-year struggle with pornography. It started when his seven-year old brain was struck with images of women in lingerie in a catalog. When he accepted Jesus, he was repentant, but the sin returned. It haunted him in his eleven-year marriage to a Christian woman. With the help of a brother in Jesus, he finally faced the problem and even confessed it to his wife, with the risk of losing her and his family. God spoke to her to love him to health, so she was a factor in his complete release from this pet sin.

The key here was the Christian brother. This man realized unless he confessed his sin to his believer friend, getting it out into the open as James 5:16 commands, He couldn't be healed. Confessing to God will bring forgiveness, but confessing to another brings *healing*.

The revelation that few have grasped of the laying down of our long-term problems and weaknesses on the new moon that occurs every month has been a cause for breakthrough for many on our blog site (search "new moon" at the A-Z section at www.freedomchurchofgod. com.) They turn over to Jesus the hardwiring of the brain that tends to bring these problems back to haunt them.

One young lady related a praise report. She had gone through the new moon taking all the things that she did while on drugs, turning them over to Jesus. She figured she should get rid of the shame and guilt that went along with the drugs. She felt so new and fresh, receiving a new start. She turned her addiction over to Jesus and all the unforgiveness, and for a month after her report she had been totally free from all draw to it. She exclaimed that Jesus was so wonderful to take such problems.

The lust, sin, and death cycle exacts its toll (James 1:15) and must be stopped because lust compromises our integrity and causes us to love evil and hate what is good. Lust causes us to speak Satan's words and even to curse God. Lust gets into our hearts to get us to love evil and sin. No one doubts God, walks in fear, or listens to lust unless they love evil in their heart. But Job turned away from evil. He persevered and eventually received all the blessings of God.

Satan doesn't want us to ask for every good and perfect gift from our Father, and he definitely doesn't want us to accept the love of our Father. That love enables us to turn our sins over to Jesus and our hearts to our Abba Father. The devil doesn't want us to walk in the joy of Jesus in good times and bad so we can receive all God wants to give us. Satan wants to destroy us, but he can't if we say no to our lusts.

Saying no to Satan ensures we will reap the blessings of the abundant life (James 1:16-18).

You are unable to ask in faith to receive all your Father of lights wants to give you unless you comprehend this colossal truth: your heavenly Father loves you so much that He is determined to bestow upon you every good gift. All you have to do is to ask for them by name and receive them in joy with a "yes and amen."

Trials come by Satan to see if you will surrender these gifts of abundance to him. He brings in doubt, double mindedness, and lust to make you ask amiss, thus looking at the gifts of God as evil.

What Do We Do with Adversity?

This study of trials brings us to discuss adversity, whose synonyms have been cited as trouble, misery, disaster, or distress. Bad things happen to people, believers or not. Adversity can be caused by our own bad choices, or it could be Satan wanting to stop us from making right choices.

Christians often speak of adversity as a friend. While trials in general can be tools for growth, we must understand that adversity is also the name of a demon that specializes in bringing bad events into our lives. As such, adversity must be resisted, even though it isn't a demon that can be sent to the pit. God has given keys as to how to defeat adversity by our words and actions so that this demon can't stay around to trouble us. Here are the twelve keys:

1. Sing.
2. Dance.
3. Shout.
4. Listen to praise and worship music.
5. Praise and thank God.
6. Read Scripture aloud and speak out the Word against the attacks.
7. Obtain and pray with prayer partners.

8. Seek the support of your church congregation.
9. Rely on the Holy Spirit.
10. Use wisdom.
11. Declare you are redeemed by Jesus' blood (because your Father loves you).
12. Laugh!

While these holy weapons will keep the spirit of adversity away, trials will inevitably come. We need to understand exactly what trials are. The spirit of adversity doesn't always bring them on. Trials are tests brought on by circumstances of cause and effect or by Satan and allowed by God. They are tests to see if we will learn lessons of character through them, and subsequent trials come to see if we have indeed learned the lessons.

Some trials are meant to be. But many Christians believe in the doctrine of demons called penance. They believe they must be punished. They condemn themselves as sinners and believe that when bad things happen to them, they deserve them. God is justly punishing them, and that punishment is something they must go through, something that will please God. For the most part, however, that isn't true.

Jesus suffered for us so we don't have to suffer. The only godly sufferings are persecution, in which we rejoice since we are becoming truly mature sons of our Father (Mat. 5:44-48), and the mental suffering that comes about when we say no to what pleases our flesh when those fleshly cravings are against God's Word and will.

People persecute us because of our love and obedience to Jesus. So why shouldn't we rejoice? We can also rejoice when other trials come, even though they may not be God's perfect will, since all things do work for our good (Rom. 8:28), and we learn from our afflictions (Ps. 119:71). We have a merciful Father, the Father of mercies and comfort (2 Cor. 1:3) who allows us to learn from our sins and mistakes.

Churches based in legalism, religiosity, judgmentalism, and perfectionism don't allow you the freedom to make mistakes and learn from them. In fact, if you don't display the same kind of perfection they pretend to have, you can't even stay in their churches. God is a God of order (1 Cor. 14:33, 40), but He allows us free will. He picks us up when we fall, and we see our Redeemer Jesus take ugly situations and make them beautiful (Gen. 50:20).

Zophar, So Good? — It's Not Always Cause and Effect!

When we go through ugly trials, the people around us, even fellow Christians are usually about as much help as Job's friends.

Ever had judgmental friends like Job? Zophar especially treated this righteous man like a joke (Job 12:4). Trite clichés instead of sincere compassion hurt like knives in our heart when we are going through something difficult. Job's friends were so caught up in religiosity that they kicked Job while he was down.

Know the feeling? You go through a grief of losing someone you love, and your religious friends tell you, "The Lord took her for a reason, and she's in heaven, so why are you so sad?" Cliches kill. Words of love—sometimes silent, listening love— bring life.

Zophar claimed that wisdom had two sides (Job 11:6). Indeed, worldly wisdom is the knowledge of good and evil that God condemned in the garden. He said not to eat of that tree. Job lambasted Zophar for his false ideas.

In Job 12:5, Job lashes out against a prevalent false doctrine expressed by Zophar and shared by both Muslims and Christians. He did, however, add a conceptual verse showing he understood that problems do sometimes come from our sins "He who is at ease holds calamity in contempt, as prepared for those whose feet slip."

When you understand the full meaning of "ease" and "contempt" (*buwz*, pronounced "booze" and having a definite connection with our word for being drunk, in this case drunk in one's pride), here is what Job was saying: "Calamities, troubles, and disasters come seeking the person who is speaking and asking in contempt and disrespect, shaming those who seek God with all their heart. They are so drunk with their own striving for self-aggrandizement, self-glorification, and haughtiness that they don't recognize a gift from God or the love of God. The powers of the pit have therefore made their way slippery and assured of a fall, for they look to money to save them and have rejected the Sabbath rest in Jesus."

But is calamity always the result of mistakes or sins on our part? The resounding answer is no.

Even if He had allowed Job to be placed in the writings rather than the prophets at the time of Solomon, Jesus knew the importance of Job's prophecies, and He affirmed them. His disciples, like the friends of Job, assumed if something bad happens to you, it has to be from sin of yours or your parents. But Jesus agreed with Job that such a concept wasn't true (John 9:1-3).

When tragedies happen, Christians either blame them on God, as if He likes to make people sick or kill them, or they blame the victim, believing they committed some horrible sin. While it is true that cause and effect are often factors, this isn't always the case.

A popular Christian singer lost his young Chinese adoptive daughter in a tragic accident. Some believed God took her so she could be with Him immediately in heaven. Others wondered what he had done to deserve this. The more likely truth is that Chinese girls are heavily cursed, often with death, and Christians don't always know about these considerations. They don't break off the curses since they don't believe curses have much power.

Hurtful Clichés versus Healing Truths

It's not always our fault that we weren't taught truths that could have saved our lives or our children's lives. And few believers really believe Jesus can raise the dead through them because they've been taught, "That was Jesus. We can't do that; we're not Jesus." Pastor haven't taught their congregations about John 14:12. Read it.

Meanwhile, Christians suffer because of lack of knowledge, and God blames the ones who should have taught them (Hos. 4:6). But other Christians more often than not blame those whom tragedy strikes, opening their big mouths with clichés that hurt like knives in a fresh wound.

Job's friends gave the typically simplistic, uncompassionate, trite, and hurtful assessments we often get from fellow Christians when we're down. "You must have sinned badly, Job, to get in this fix," was their attitude. With friends like some religious people who play a role of knowing God when they don't know him intimately, who needs enemies?

When problems and tragedies come, it's not always because we sinned. It's time we quit judging and understand why some bad things happen to some good people. Here are some possibilities:

- A direct attack by demons.
- Wrong prayers by a person not moving in love but in legalism, witchcraft, fear, control, and unforgiveness. Just recently I was unable to sleep because some who thought they were doing a good deed were praying for me in fear. I had expressed need for prayers regarding my sleep. God doesn't answer prayers of fear or prayers to "the Lord," but Satan does.
- Betrayal by a friend, mate, family member, or a church.
- Curses that haven't been rejected. I suffered with pain and discomfort for three weeks before I realized it came from being cursed by a religious person that didn't like my dancing at a conference in a session of songs of praise.
- Backlash for moving on something without having full understanding or protection. Not being taught isn't a sin.
- Generational curses that manifest in the third or fourth generation. Why would we be responsible for a sin of our grandfather? We may face the consequence but don't bear the guilt.
- Incantations, spells, hexes, talismans, etc. sent by witches.
- Terrors, traumas, and nightmares that haven't been understood and turned over to Jesus. Jesus' shed His blood seven times to free us from traumas, but how many Christians know about what He did and the freedom He paid for?

- Having wrong prophecies spoken over us and accepted without realizing their importance.
- Being labeled by people without our direct knowledge. I only realized I had been labeled with a serious label by some members in France, one that affected me for thirty years before I was able to break it off.
- Having others attach their souls to us without our knowledge.
- Having numerous soul ties, blood bonds and vows affecting and tormenting our soul.
- Being rejected for the Word of God or the light of God being manifested in our life. Jesus warned us of persecution by family.
- Not recognizing the times, seasons, or the days we are in.
- Praying to the Lord rather than to the Father in Jesus' name, thus allowing the spirit of quagmire to push us from one ditch to the other.

Victory in Trials

God knows in advance every trial that will befall us, whatever the cause may be, and He always provides a way out of the trial (1 Cor. 10:13). But He wants us to go through the test with our hands in Jesus' hands to walk us through the valley (Ps. 23:4). And James continues to tell us what lessons God wants us to learn.

We are to learn to be slow to anger in a trial (James 1:19-20). When we look at everyone and everything through the eyes of anger, we can't walk in love but are burdened by legalism and judgmentalism. We aren't in a position to receive from Father Love.

James repeats some of his warnings in this paraphrase: "You lust and don't have; so you commit your heart to the spirit of murder; and you are envious and can't obtain; so you fight, gossip, undermine, murmur, seduce, lie, destroy, and quarrel. You don't have because you don't ask in love. And when you do ask and don't receive, it's because you ask with wrong, lustful, murdering motives so that you may spend, consume, and employ it on your sin-filled pleasures" (James 5:2-3).

Nothing can be given us when we ask for it in the spirit of murder, fear, or lust. Job prayed and sacrificed in fear for his children (Job 1:5) and his fears came true (Job 3:25).

James gives us keys to receiving the gifts of God as we go through the trials that prepare us to receive: " But He [Father Love] gives a greater gift of empowerment. Therefore it is written, 'God is opposed to the proud who love murder and lust, but He gives the empowerment to the humble, teachable, and contrite. Submit therefore to God. Resist the devil, and he will flee from you. Draw near to God in love, truth, and faith, and He will draw near to you. Cleanse your hands, you lovers of evil and sin, and purify your hearts, you who choose fear and double mindedness" (James 4:6-8, paraphrased).

As did David, Job asked a lot of questions of God because he truly wanted to know Him and His ways, but he submitted to God and turned away from evil (Job 1:8). He resisted the devil, so Satan in the end had to flee from him. As we stay steadfast in trials, he will also flee from us, no matter how much he wants to destroy us in his end-time wrath (Rev. 12:10-12).

Job said the slave would one day be free from his master (Job 3:19), and James tells us how: "But as it is, you boast in your arrogance, pretentions, and fantasies. All such boasting is evil. Therefore, to one who knows the ways of God, to do the right thing, and yet does not do it, to him it is sin" (James 4:16-17).

The master in this world is Satan, the lord of boasting, arrogance, pretentions, and fantasies of aggrandizement. Death will set us free of his pressures over us, but God has another way, a way that gives us life in real peace, love, abundance, and freedom. We can block it and be bound to Satan and his demons in marriage, or we can embrace it and be married to Jesus in eternal life and the gifts of our Father Love. The question is: Will we allow our trials to prepare us to receive the wonderful gifts of God?

"Where did Your love go?" That's the questions too many believers ask of their Father. They forget that His name is Love, and He can't help loving us. He's not there to make problems for us, but He is our great Problem Solver. He allows trials so we'll look to Him for help. He wants us to trust Him as we go through the valleys. Those who persevere in these trials of the last days will be ultimately saved, if they don't give up on God (Mat. 24:13).

Satan wants to wear down the saints, but our Father encourages us not to lose heart in doing good, "...for in due time we will reap if we do not grow weary" (Gal. 6:9). Will you allow Satan to wear you down and out? Will you be mad at your Father for allowing trials in your life, or will you praise and thank Him that He will bring you through?

Some end-time believers will be given into the hands of a satanic leader for three and a half years (Dan. 7:25). The Roswell Stone gives the same time frame. This leader will wage war with the saints, "... overpowering them" (Dan. 7:21). Not all will be overpowered. Some will shine (Dan. 12:3). Some will trust Jesus to qualify them to take possession of the Kingdom of God, ruling with Jesus on this earth soon. If you turn your heart to Father Love in these last days, even amid all the trials, you will be of their number (Dan. 7:22; Rev. 5:10). How much do you want to receive that reward?

CHAPTER 7

The Promise of Faith

We have seen the power of knowing God loves us. The Bible says that faith works by love (Gal. 5:6), so we should have a good foundation in love, a key to reaching the Father's heart. That brings us, however, to another question our apostle answered in one of his insightful sermons from the Holy Spirit that we relate here.

Where is your faith's foundation? Many believe it is in the grace of there being no more sin. The law is done away, the words of the prophets mean nothing, and Satan is powerless to tempt or corrupt anything.

Also many believe in a man, the pope, to be vicar of the world. In him alone comes all righteousness and forgiveness. And in him goes forth the truths of God's Word to the world. Not good.

There are many who seek the wisdom of the stars for making decisions on what should happen in their life. They have no understanding of how they mock God's love. Again, not good.

There are those who rely on rituals, traditions, and ordinances that were made by men who were in love with sin. They stay bound to fears, guilt, and shame and thus never experience the freedom of the new day. Freedom and life stays far away from them. Definitely, not good.

And a great many believe that rocks, metal, and trees have a greater life and validity than God the Father, Jesus, and the Holy Spirit combined. Statues, gold and silver, cement structures and positions have more knowledge, truth and, wisdom than God. Totally, not good.

So where is your foundation of faith? Are you a believer whose faith is built upon Jesus being your God and Savior? Do you see yourself playing a role to look good or one who trusts Jesus and lives their life in the grace of love? Do you know the Word and does the Word know you? The promises of God are about to catch you if you really know Jesus.

What would shake your faith? What would make you think that God is against you? Could it be…?

- A flat tire.
- Your job.
- Your church.
- Your bank.
- A missed television show.
- A broken television
- An unexpected visitor.
- Losing your favorite pen.
- Being robbed.
- Another's sin that you heard about.
- Not having your future mate to bed by Friday night.
- Having to go through a test, a trial, a temptation.
- Having to live for a while in bad circumstances.
- Finding out you were living in sin by your judgments, condemnations, and evaluations of others.
- Being labeled as lazy, incompetent, or a whiner.
- Finding out your best friend calls you damaged goods or a slut.
- Being made to suffer because of another's sin.
- Being raped by someone you trusted.
- Misplacing your Bible that you haven't seen or read for over two years.
- Being evicted from your home.
- Finding unclean food in your kosher dinner.
- Having all the things you fear attack you—all in the same week
- A slight delay in getting a promise from God.
- Having all your hidden secrets published by others for the world to see and condemn you for.

- Being lied about by the press and TV, church, and family.
- A close friend borrowing money and not repaying it.
- Someone you have trusted with a secret tells everybody what you did.
- The sleeping giants return from Noah's day.

Once we can acknowledge and face the things that shake our faith, we can start receiving the promises that come from faith. We can put aside the things of childhood and grow into the maturity of sons. When we turn over what shakes our faith, we can ask for the empowerment to defeat what steals our faith.

So then what is faith? Faith is like a beautifully cut diamond. It becomes polished as we use it the way intended. We all have our basic measure of faith or we couldn't exist. We have to have this basic measure of faith that says to us that we exist and *existence exists*. As we meet pressures, trials, temptations, and challenges in life we grow in our basic faith. When we die to ourselves and let the Holy Spirit and Jesus live in us, then we establish ourselves for travel on the path that can lead us up to the tenth level of faith. Yet at each level we have to establish ourselves into a deeper relationship with Jesus in order to produce the confidence to use faith at the new level.

However, when we want to have the faith of the believer, we have to work the foundations for making faith, for activating faith, and for causing it to grow.

Foundation # 1: A belief that God exists

This sounds all too simple but it is the very cause as to why a person never becomes a strong believer. The concept of belief is to not ask the questions of doubt, asking what God is doing in your life and why He is doing something that doesn't agree with your paradigm. Our faith can't grow without horrendous pain beyond our desire to establish questions. The question of, "why, God why?", is the very key Satan uses in getting us to take off our armor and let Satan steal and destroy whatever faith we do have. Our ability to believe what God is saying to us is corrupted every time we use the key, "why, God, why," and thus growth is stopped.

Belief says that God is in charge and that He knows what we need to grow into becoming sons of God. It is our *heart* agreement that established belief that makes faith-growth possible. When our heart can't get past the why, our faith shrivels until we die because even our faith in our existence becomes too small to sustain physical life.

Foundation # 2 Trust

Trust is to know that God can change all things and do all things for our good and for our best results.

Trust needs belief to be established first before it will work. Trust doesn't need the answers as to when, how, or what if. Trust says that God is good and that God will always do what is best for me at the right time. Trust says that God knows the beginning from the end. He knows when I am ready to receive, to move forward, and when my confidence level needs adjusting.

Trust relies on the promises of God and it rests in these promises. It also relies on God's purpose and God's vision for our life. Trust employs the talents God has given us to grow and to help others. When we walk in trust we glorify God and avoid flaunting ourselves.

Foundation # 3: Zeal

This zeal is a zeal for God, His ways, and His laws.

Zeal implies a desire for Jesus, a desire to be like Him, and an excitement at knowing that you can have it. The word used in Hebrew is *qana*, which is to make zealous, to be jealous in defense of, to have an envy of, to love people so much that you live to serve them and to please them with your whole heart, mind, and strength.

A zeal for God implies that zealous love or jealous love for every Word of God, every precept, every concept, every law, every ordinance, and every judgment of God. You put it into your heart and you protect it against every attempt that Satan makes to steal, pollute, compromise, or seduce it. And you do this out of love for God and everything He says.

Psalms 119: 138-140 says, "You have commanded Your testimonies in righteousness and exceeding faithfulness. My zeal has consumed me, because my adversaries have forgotten Your words. Your word is very pure, therefore, Your servant loves it."

These verses from Psalm 119 establish the foundation of zeal faith. They explain that God is exceedingly faithful to His Word. So He speaks what is right and He defends His Word. He keeps His Word and He acknowledges the love of those who seek to keep it and obey it. David said that his zeal for the Word consumed him or we could say that it changed him from selfishness to faithful love. Because the Word of God is so very pure, David said he could do nothing but love it.

Zeal-faith also means that you seek to feed your soul from *no other source*.

Foundation #4 Gratitude

Gratitude employs thankfulness, and it is cumulative in nature. It is like a diary in which we keep an ever-growing list of the things Jesus has done in our life and in the lives of others. And we remind our Father Love of all the things He has done.

The lack of gratitude causes a lack of faith in the promises of God, in our ability to get free from sin, in our desire to bless others, and in our ability to give.

When we examine a part of Psalm 119:67-72 we see gratitude as a concept of faith.

David wrote, "Before I was afflicted, I went astray, but now I keep Your word" (Ps. 119:67). David was grateful that Jesus spent time to discipline him so that he could learn the Word of God. He was grateful that the Word of God came alive to him in times of affliction.

David continued, "You are good and your purpose is good; teach me Your statutes" (Ps. 119:68).

Here David expressed gratitude that Jesus is good and seeks to do good in our lives. *This concept is so important* in building faith that until we acknowledge that God's purpose is for our good only, our faith will always falter. And then our words become doubts and questions of how and why God does what He does. They are always on our heart and on our tongue. Fear sets in to grow.

"The arrogant have forged a lie against me; with all my heart, I will observe Your precepts" (Ps. 119:69). David knew that the precepts of God's Word would save him and correct the effects of any lie. Liars hate God's truth and those who seek to live godly lives. The keeping of God's Word breaks the power of lies.

David continued, " Their heart is covered with fat, but I delight in Your law" (Ps. 119:70). The wicked or arrogant seek security in riches, things, and power. David said the delight of his heart was anchored in the law of God. He was grateful that he had God's law to guide his activities so that he didn't have to rely on the get system and its turmoil to become rich. He was grateful that he was blessed.

In verse 71 David wrote, "It is good for me that I was afflicted, that I may learn Your statutes." Again David expresses gratitude for the lessons learned in affliction. The discipline of God made him receptive to changing and gave him a willingness and purpose in learning God's statutes. It set his heart from war to the ways of peace and truth.

Then he exclaimed, "The law of your mouth is better to me than thousands of gold and silver pieces" (Ps. 119:72). David expresses gratitude for getting to know Jesus before he was corrupted by wealth and the get system.

From these verses we see that our faith levels grow more quickly when we call for gratitude to be our guide in staying close to Jesus. Faith can't be maintained if gratitude doesn't come out of our tongue or mouth. The gratitude-faith foundation allows the promises of God to flow without blockage.

Foundation #5: Hope

There are two types of hope. The most popular one is what the churches teach. It is a wish that is part of witchcraft. It expresses a love of events and things that don't line up with the Word of God. It also becomes the foundation for lust to grab a person's heart.

The hope of God is the least popular of all types of hope because it requires faith in God and in His Word. It requires steadfastness and a love of the truth. This hope requires faith to be sown as a seed to grow into more mature levels of faith. Hope doesn't and won't put limits on God. The hope of God can employ the faith of God to do anything. And Jesus spoke out the conditions for God's hope and faith to work.

We find them in Genesis 11:6: " Behold, they are one people, and they all have the same language. And this is what they began to do and *nothing* which they purpose to do will be impossible for them."

Unity as one people, speaking one language with one purpose and one vision is impossible to stop. When people employ faith and hope as their foundation, nothing is impossible for them to achieve.

Foundation # 6: Patience

In patience we find a concept of perseverance without whining, sympathy seeking, or murmuring. Faith-patience allows you to meditate on the things of God and not the oppression of the moment. It makes you see God first, and nothing else is your priority.

Luke 21: 14-19 needs to be read and deeply dwelt upon in order to understand the faith-patience foundation: "So make up your minds not to prepare beforehand to defend yourselves; *for* I will give you utterance and wisdom which none of your opponents will be able to resist or refute. But you will be betrayed even by parents and brothers and relatives and friends, and they will put some of you to death, and you will be hated by *all* [peoples, demons] because of My name. Yet not a hair of your head will perish. By your endurance [patience, perseverance] you will gain your lives."

Your desire to focus on God the Father instead of what people are doing to you is not just a waiting type of focus. It is active in praising and forgiving. Then your thoughts dwell on Jesus and not on people and the things that they do. Your patience consists in not complaining, not cursing and not trying to earn your own favor with a persecutor. This attitude will cause their souls to seek Jesus because this patience-faith is a God-trained faith.

Foundation # 7: Truth

The concept of truth is very hard for most people to accept or even hold onto. David said that the Word of God is truth. God cannot lie; therefore every word He says is truth. Yet we are to have a faith-truth in our minds and hearts. It is written, "prove all things, hold fast to those things which are true." A faith-truth requires that we have godly knowledge, wisdom, and understanding so that we discern truth from the lies and deception.

Psalm 25:5 says," Lead me in Your truth and teach me, for You are the God of my salvation: for You I wait all the day." The foundation of faith-truth is a trained and taught procedure and it takes time to develop.

We read in Psalm 25:10 "All the paths of the [Eternal] are lovingkindness and truth to those who keep His covenant and His testimonies."

You need to be teachable to learn truth and be able to prove truth so that you can hold onto it. And when you keep and practice what you know, the power of God is released through you, because Faith has promised to act.

We bless you with a heart that seeks all the foundations of faith. In Jesus' name.

CHAPTER 8

Lack of Knowledge Can Kill!

Today I was watching the Christian Broadcasting Network daily program, and I was struck by an interview with a Christian counselor and his wife who had lost their young son to cancer. They had prayed for healing and were devastated by this tragedy. He counseled many people in similar circumstances, but he never knew for himself the pain that it caused.

As they talked about their gut wrenching experience, they were understandably emotional about their battle with understanding why God allowed such pain. They thought they had done everything right and deserved to have everything go right in their lives. She said to God, "This doesn't feel like love. You're supposed to be loving."

The pain and trauma in their voices made it clear to me that they had never been released from trauma's pain, nor had they laid down to Jesus the enormous pain they had gone through.

The thought came to me, how could their hearts turn fully and completely to the Father in these last days when their hearts are hurting still from feeling betrayed by that Father. It occurred to me that the work of Satan, stealing and destroying the knowledge that sets free, has succeeded in keeping people from reaching the Father's heart.

The knowledge about trauma and about the new moon where long-term pains are surrendered to Jesus is indeed available, but Satan has kept it from getting to the majority of Christians. God gave mankind, and that includes Christians, free will. He can't alter that decision that

He made. He doesn't want robots but men and women who have built character by choosing life and truth.

Sadly, Satan has stolen so much of the truth. Those who are blessed to dispense it are often maligned, rejected, or ignored. So as Hosea said, God's people have been destroyed for lack of knowledge.

The knowledge and power to raise the dead has been given to the church, but most are so doubtful and fearful about such an action that they wouldn't even try. Healing is a promise, but few Christians know how to claim it and eliminate by God's grace the hindrances to receiving that healing.

It's a sad state of affairs.

We see tragedy after tragedy among believers in Jesus who don't have to be affected by tragedies. But there are so many experiencing these horrible circumstances that most Christians have resigned to believing tragedy is part of life and just accept it.

You don't have to accept tragedy. By speaking and living the Word of God and taking regular, enlightened communion, you can receive God's protection in these calamitous times.

God meets people in His mercy where they are, and He does comfort them in their afflictions and struggles. All things do indeed work for good in their lives if they allow it, even tragedy.

We posted our YouTube video about major storms, including hurricane Sandy in 2012, and one of our viewers insisted we were wrong in stating that these storms didn't come from God but from Satan. He stated that Christians die of tragedies all the time. I encouraged him to read the miracles of protection throughout the Bible. Normal behavior and occurrences for Christians is not necessarily normal in God's book. He promises to protect us, so the problem isn't with God but with us.

Satan has robbed us of understanding God's Word. We are surrounded by a faithless society that rubs off on us if we are not vigilant. And over nine thousand doctrines of demons that have polluted the churches have destroyed us for lack of understanding the truths of God's Word.

People, even Christians, speak words of death: "I'm scared to death." They speak these words because of a secret but willful longing for death.

Missing dear relatives who die and missing them to the point of wanting to be with them causes us to seek death, not life, and this longing should be laid down to Jesus on the new moon. Many believers die too early because of hanging onto death in this way.

God's desire is to restore all that knowledge in the last days. We pray for the accomplishment of His perfect will, yet we also realize His will depends to some degree on the loyalty of His servants.

If believers are to return to the Father's heart of love in this end time, they must turn over their feelings of pain, unforgiveness, and betrayal to Jesus. We must not allow these negative feelings to govern our relationship with Father Love.

CHAPTER 9

Sex and the Father-hating Syndrome

"*Sex and the Single Girl*" was a book and a movie in the early 1960's. We believers know that sex outside of marriage is sin. But could sex in marriage be sin? The answer is yes. It occurs many times with a husband in the father-hating syndrome who doesn't prepare his wife for the act of marriage by showing love. He rapes her.

Our society deluges us with a media blitz that cries, "Get sex now!" Sex is everywhere, except where it should be, as an act of true love and sharing in a marriage blessed by God. A husband's love and kindness toward his wife makes her a willing and joyous partner in a holy sexual union. Sadly, such a relationship is rare—especially in a marriage where the husband hates his father.

We have had a deluge of comments about a syndrome we have now called the father-hating syndrome, extreme unforgiveness of a son to his father. One of the excellent contributors to our site is an experienced counselor who has dealt with the problem from a personal and professional perspective. He put his finger on one of the main motivations of the man in this syndrome: he evaluates everyone and everything from the standpoint of sex. This is one of the many facets of the spirit of lust, which is a problem of father-haters.

This doesn't always mean that if the person wouldn't be an interesting sex partner, he wants nothing to do with them. The brain contains a sexual center that doesn't always give direct sexual pleasure, but the satisfaction received is a pleasant one that stimulates this part of the brain.

Women who have been married to such men have commented and asked questions on Freedom Blog. We applaud most of the advice given by our experienced bloggers, with one exception—the frying pan on the head solution. We suggest wives of abusive husbands in this syndrome do something that gets the attention of their husbands. Each situation is different, and listening to the Holy Spirit for your unique problem is essential.

Till Divorce Do Them Part?

In some cases, the free will of the father hater allows no other solution than divorce, according to the biblical stipulations. If you decide on divorce, don't feel guilty. The Bible provides guidelines for divorce and remarriage on the basis of God's Word. We have a complete article on the subject, "Divorce and Remarriage," in the A-Z section of freedomchurchofgod.com.

We share with our readers some of the blog entries that have brought about a lively discussion. Here is one of the questions: One lady asked what a woman should do when she's not ready for sex but does it anyway. She believes that's what God wants, so that she's not withholding sex from her husband. Then she's screaming in her head while it's going on because of the pain. What does God want these women to do? She didn't believe He wants them to suffer in order to fulfill the desires of their husbands' flesh. Is there a length of time they're allowed to not have sex with their husband, she asked. But then must they have sex again or else be disobeying God even if it hurts them, she asked?

Our most inspired blogger, a lady who has since passed away replied that when a man can't hold himself together until his mate is ready for sex, [he] is 100% stuck in the [father-hating] condition. She encouraged the requester to declare her boundaries, her times of need and what conditions she needed in order for you to be prepared to maximize her enjoyment of sex and that of her husband. If she felt that she could handle sex only once or twice a week, then she should tell him. If he refuses to listen, then she was encouraged to do something to get his attention.

Another woman added excellent advice: the question is really stating how far is a wife expected to serve, to love and to share? The key factor is whether it interferes with a wife's time and walk with God and the time needed to teach and look after the children. This blogger encouraged this lady to set her heart on enjoying her husband, and the pain would quickly disappear.

We add that your pain will disappear if he has respected your boundaries. In such cases, you can prepare yourself for the act of marriage, and he is thus making changes that will show more love and thus prepare you for the act. You will be released from the fear of rape, which will allow no woman to be ready for mutually enjoyable sex.

Jesus had various ways of getting the attention of his errant Israelite bride before He had to divorce her, without the frying pan on the head solution. God uses wisdom and wants us to act in wisdom and love.

Jesus once told Abraham to listen to his wife when Sarah told him to get rid of Hagar (Gen. 21:11-13). But sometimes when husbands don't listen after repeated efforts, it's time to administer some tough love. If and when they repent and you don't have to divorce them with biblical foundation, they will thank you.

Such actions of tough love must be bathed in prayer and guided by the Holy Spirit. Whatever you decide on, it must be something that really gets the attention of your husband. Some have used unannounced, unofficial separations as a measure that got some attention. Others have had to call for legal separations, hoping to avoid a divorce. However, the free will of the husband sometimes makes divorce inevitable.

It's No Use Taking Abuse

Abusive husbands need a wake-up call. They tend to think they are such wonderful husbands, all the while having no love for their wives, whom they rape repeatedly. These husbands may be as blinded as some Muslim men who have claimed that no such thing as rape exists in marriage. One father-hater stated to this pastor, "I don't 'have sex' with my wife. I 'make love'." But that wasn't what his wife said, and it wasn't the truth. She spent much time in persistent prayer before going for divorce.

The Bible gives general guidelines of how a wife is supposed to honor her husband, but husbands that abuse their wives have lost the respect they should have earned, and in such cases, they do not fit into the category of respectable. You respect the office, but not the man. And sometimes winning them "without a word" (1 Pet. 3:1) may mean some drastic action, tailored to fit your man.

After all, you're dealing with a mate who is showing by his actions that he is not truly pleased to dwell with his wife in peace (1 Cor. 7:13-15), so you have biblical grounds for divorce.

The Jesus who hates divorce had to divorce Israel (Mal. 2:16; Jer. 3:8). No woman wants this, but after gentle love and tough love have not worked, sometimes it's the only solution. We hope this advice can save some marriages on the brink. But as our experienced blog answerers always do, soak everything in prayer. God never overrides free will, but Jesus can redeem any situation.

Whatever the outcome, even divorce, we pray God's blessing of wisdom, redemption, and restored lives for the wives of father-haters. Even if your husbands choose not to be victors in this life, you are more than conquerors (Rom. 8:37-39), and no power on earth, even an abusive husband, can separate you from the love of God.

The Father-hater as Sex Addict

Sex is a hot topic today. Satan wants it so, since his perversion of this wonderful gift from God in marriage is one of his major weapons in these last days. He knows that he can have permission to bring back the flesh and sex-hungry giants as in the days of Noah (Mat. 24:37).

God foreknew that the great need in the last days would be for a son to forgive his father so he could forgive Father God (Mal. 4:6). God knew that this unforgivness would cause sex addiction that would open big doors for Satan and the possible destruction of all mankind and humankind as in the days of Noah.

God gives the only real solution to sex addiction in James 5:16. Don't keep it secret. Tell a trusted friend, and you open the door to healing, not only God's forgiveness.

The father-hating syndrome can also apply to hatred of an older brother, and women can also have this syndrome with somewhat different symptoms than men. We have seen, however, that it is principally masculine father haters who become addicts whose motto seems to be, "get sex now," with no regard to the readiness of their wives.

In our sex-crazed society singles and married folk alike seem to have forgotten that sex is not a need but a desire. God does say that it belongs as a blessing He ordains and protects in marriage. This glorious gift from God has a number of purposes when used in the blessed marital union.

In *Uncovered*, author Susie Davis quotes Megan K. Scott in a *Seattle Times* article in presenting several possible purposes God intended for sex in marriage. They are: to create life; for intimate oneness; for personal, intimate knowledge of one another; for pleasure (God is not a prude); as a defense against temptation (I Cor. 7:5); and for comfort.

The father hater sex addict would only agree with a few of these. He loves to create babies as trophies of his sexual prowess without a desire to truly love those children. He wants the pleasure part, but only for himself, no matter how pious a Christian father hater may claim to be. He may boast that he doesn't have sex but makes love. In reality, he makes love with himself. He does so either in masturbation or in his selfish fantasies as he treats his wife like a sex doll in which he deposits his seed while thinking of who he is really lusting for at the time.

Divorce and the Cloak of Invisibility

His wife is rendered invisible. The *cloak of invisibility* (search for this at www.freedomchurchofgod.com) is probably the main reason for marital break-ups. Experienced marriage and sex counselors have explored areas like anorexia addiction, meaning that mates purposely starve their mates of love, or marital independence, where mates act independently and without the knowledge of the other. In both of these cases, however, the root is invisibility. Both syndromes cause the mate to feel invisible. Counseling can bring improvements; however, unless we realize that our fight is with unseen forces (Eph. 6:12), in this case a spiritual cloak of invisibility that Satan has been allowed to put over the marriage, the roots will remain.

The sex addict believes that comfort is one of God's reasons for sex. Oh yes, he likes the comfort, but only for himself. Sex relieves him of the illicit desires that are pent up in him by giving himself to the temptation of undressing in his brain every halfway good-looking woman he sees.

He evaluates everyone and everything according to the sexual pleasure he thinks he can derive, and the more contempt he shows toward a person, the less the sexual value he sees. That is one sign of a sex addiction, which can be defined as Satan's method of temporary relief from pain of the past, especially a sense of loss in your life. Lust, lying, selfishness, and fear support the spirit of addictions. A sex addict is constantly seeking to relieve his past pain with various forms of sexual fulfillment rather than turning over all the pain to Jesus.

They don't prepare their wives for the sexual encounter, thus committing what is tantamount to rape, which brings sin into the bedroom and invites Satan in (Heb. 13:4). They run down their mates in other areas so the wife feels like she is only begrudgingly kept as a sex toy.

One of our members who had to divorce her husband put it this way: "They say that you owe them sex for everything. Whenever you make a mistake you have to make it up to them through sex. Whenever they make a mistake you need to make them feel better by having sex with them. Whenever they feel aroused (which is pretty much always) you have to have sex with them. Whenever they lust after someone or something, it's always your fault for not having sex with them enough, not 'fulfilling your God-given obligation.'"

She also relates how their unforgiveness creates spiritual blindness: "They really like to say, 'I'm sorry you're so wrong and mixed up. I'll let you make it up to me through sex,' or else they'll apologize for their weaknesses, say they're going to try harder, and twist the (one-sided) conversation around so that whatever the issue was, it's your fault for not having enough sex with them. Essentially, they say 'I'm so sorry. I'm really a great guy. Everyone else knows that, but these bad things happen because of you.' Or they say, 'I'm sorry. It's all your fault, but I know you can do better' … they want an excessive amount of sex, so that there is no time left for anything else."

CHAPTER 10

Doctrines That Turn Us Away from the Father's Heart

Satan hates the idea of our hearts turning to Father Love. He has done and is doing everything he can to stop the fulfillment of Malachi 4:6, since his victory would bring about the destruction of all life on earth. The destroyer would love to see this, but your reading and understanding of this book can destroy him and his plans. You can be a part of the fulfillment of an end-time mission that will bring about a reformation and revival that Satan will hate even more.

Satan has deceived the whole world (Rev. 12:9), but his greatest deception is within the visible church. When he couldn't win from the outside, he went inside. His inside job, if you can call it that, when using a pagan emperor who had a fake conversion, began with constantly compromising Constantine. Satan used him to render Christianity pagan. He introduced over five thousand doctrines of demons in the visible church, the number of which has now grown to over nine thousand.

These doctrines keep believers from turning their hearts to a Father whose character and reputation of love has been smeared and assassinated with lies—lies that have been accepted without biblical examination by most Christians today.

The popular view of some is that Jesus is either a powerless baby in a manger or a weak, effeminate, long-haired rebel against a harsh, Old

Testament Father, and Father Love is characterized as what many would call "a fickle and cruel Indian giver."

That's a lie. It's a perversion, a twisting of what the Bible really says. Yet Satan inspires the preachers to misuse verses and says, "Preach it!" And it seems the whole Christian world chimes in the same phrase with a hearty amen. Our Father is painted as a cruel, capricious tyrant, and we swallow the lie. After all, how could all those preachers be wrong?

That's why Jesus' main warning to his end-time disciples was this: "See to it that no one misleads you" (Mat. 24:4). Let's see how Satan, the god of death, has twisted a verse used repeatedly at funerals to make us think our Father of life loves to take life away. Don't buy it.

The Most Twisted Text—The Hearse Verse

What is the most twisted verse in the Bible? It is probably the verse we choose to call the hearse verse, Job 1:21. We normally use the correct translations in our writings, but for good reason this time we'll leave in the wrong term for Jesus or God: "The LORD gave and the LORD has taken away. Blessed be the name of the LORD."

"The Lord" may take the life of your baby girl through sickness or an accident, but the true God won't, " for the gifts and the calling of God are irrevocable" (Rom. 11:29). Although some Christian songs may say that God gives and takes away, it's a lie. He is Love.

How can our hearts be turned to our Father Love if we believe lies about Him that are supposedly from the Bible? How many want to turn their hearts over to a cruel tyrant who flippantly and capriciously causes those we love to die early? Doctrines of demons often portray God as One who resembles the leader of the demons rather than a God of infinite love who is a Giver, not a Taker.

Translators have twisted this verse to glorify death and make God out to be a cruel ogre whose word no one can trust. This twisting has probably kept more Christians from being ready to meet Jesus than any other verse, and that is why we include the truth about this verse in this book.

Our God doesn't bless you with someone or something and then snatch it away from you to make you cry. God is the great Giver. It was Adam's sin that gave the devil legal right to take blessings away from us. Only Satan and his demons come to kill, steal, and destroy (John 10:10). Jesus came to give us life, not death.

When God showed us the power of the name of Jesus versus Lord (Acts 4:12), we began to see in our ministry freedom for Christians who stopped calling Jesus Lord and called him by His name. The Holy Spirit identified for us a demon named quagmire who calls himself Lord. This spirit of quagmire causes those who call on the Lord almost exclusively to go from one ditch to the other and be left in a quagmire caused by speaking words of death, not life.

This wrong translation completely misses the intention of the original, conceptual Hebrew words *nathan* (give) and *laqach* (take). Those of you who are bilingual know that sometimes one word just won't do when you try to translate words as in Job 1:21. In the original, conceptual, biblical Hebrew, sometimes as many as two hundred words are necessary.

Here is an amplified but more faithful translation of this verse; it is necessary to convey the multiple meanings: "The Eternal God has added to another for bestowing favor, opportunity, and provision, that He may bring forth the best in them, causing events to change for the better, thus authorizing provision and protection for the future king that will sow without failure, causing those He touches to fasten themselves to the ways of God and thus pouring out love, gifts, life, blood, and the Holy Spirit to all, for the Eternal God has accepted all I have as a donation, offering, and praise in cleansing every evil to make a new world fully restored to Him."

Job was saying that whatever God had given him he would use only as a steward for God. When God wanted it, he would gladly release it back to Him. He made no claim to his possessions, but he did lay claim to the future Kingdom of God and his position in it.

Christians have been blocked from being ready to marry Jesus when He calls His bride up in a rapture for many reasons. One is the misunderstanding of this verse. Because they see God as a whimsical, fickle Father who comes like Satan to steal, kill, and destroy His own children, they cannot see themselves as loved by God. Who could see themselves loved by a cruel God? Knowing our identity as beloved sons of our Father Love and brothers of Jesus is paramount, if we want to be ready to meet Jesus. But that's not the only thing.

The "Just Accept Jesus" Lie

It seems that the Baptists are one of the few churches that teach the necessity of baptism. But that's what the Bible teaches, and that's why many Christians are still walking in their old ways and are not being prepared to marry Jesus. "Just accept Jesus and you have it made. You don't need to do anything else. Everything else is works and law. Just believe, and you will be saved." But that is a doctrine of demons.

Read it for yourself in Acts 2:38. Read Jesus' own words: "He who has believed and has been *baptized* shall be saved..." (Mark 16:16).

Consider also what Jesus told John the Baptist when he initially refused to baptize Jesus: "Permit it at this time; for in this way it is fitting for us to fulfill all righteousness" (Mat. 3:15). Jesus said that baptism must be permitted. He had to show the example so that all believers would fulfill all righteousness, opening the door to having Jesus live fully in them, wearing His coat of righteousness. Jesus was saying, "This is the way or the door that everyone who will follow Me must go through." Everyone who would live in righteousness must be baptized.

If we say no to baptism, we are saying that we want to keep "the old man" that we are supposed to crucify and bury with Jesus. How else can we be raised in newness of life (Rom. 6:1-18)? You can't be raised from the dead until you die.

The movie *Dead Man Walking* comes to mind. Do we want to live the Christian life like a zombie, like a man on death row, or do we want to truly live? How can the new life in Jesus' righteousness truly begin in us if we have not surrendered our "old man" of sin? Death and life don't go together.

Some claim that we must only be baptized in Jesus' name. But Jesus Himself commanded more. He said we were to baptize disciples into the name of all three members of the Godhead (Mat. 28:19). Jesus set the example in being baptized, even though He had no sin and no old man to bury. After being immersed, Jesus heard His Father speak audibly in the hearing of mankind for the first time in history, saying proudly, "This is My beloved Son, in whom I am well-pleased" (Mat. 3:17).

How can we receive the same affirmation if we aren't baptized into the name of the Father as well as into the name of Jesus and the Holy Spirit? Every person who has ever lived is destined one day to have the opportunity to be named after the Father as a son or daughter of Love (Eph. 3:15; 1 John 4:8). Jesus said we were to honor both Him and His Father (John 5:23). How can we do that if we are only baptized in Jesus' name?

CHAPTER 11

Judgment From the Mercy Seat

How much mercy do you deserve? A thimble full? A teaspoon full? A cup full? A fifty-gallon tank full? Or a lifetime full? Some churches are so condemning that they claim that you deserve no mercy. So which one is right and how much should you claim? The answer is simple. None of these is correct.

We often get the correct answers from the Holy Spirit through our apostle, Gerald Budzinski, and we give him full credit, which He always gives to the Holy Spirit, who inspired this book. This chapter is from one of those inspired sermons.

Many define mercy as an unmerited pardon but even that is not the best definition of mercy. Jesus said something in Matthew 5:11 "Blessed are you when men revile you and persecute you, and say all kinds of evil against you falsely for My sake."

How we handle persecution for Jesus' sake becomes a key to understanding how we build mercy in our heavenly account. How do you react to being cursed at? Lied about? Falsely accused? Gossiped about? Having innuendos issued against you? Publicly maligned? Publically ridiculed? Undermined? Publicly humiliated? Or publically condemned?

Matthew 5:11 tells us how: "*Rejoice* and be exceedingly glad, for great is your reward in heaven, for so they persecuted the prophets who were before you." The reward of mercy becomes greater as you rejoice and become glad. Persecution makes you stronger while rejoicing increases your reward. Mercy is not a bottomless pit of supply unless we sow the seeds for it.

Jesus also said in Matthew 5: 7, "Blessed are the merciful for they shall receive mercy." You must sow mercy into the lives of others before mercy can be shown to you. This means that our Father sowed the initial gift of mercy into us as seed to be sown to others. You cannot grow in mercy unless you sow mercy. We shall now see the types of mercy.

Type 1—Compassion

This type is where God causes men to give us favor. He puts us in a special light to cause men to want to do good for us and to us.

In Genesis 43:14, we see the compassion-favor type put to use: "And may God Almighty grant you compassion [favor-mercy] in the sight of the man, that he may release to you your other brother and Benjamin."

Jacob was asking Jesus to cause judgment to change a mind so that mercy-favor would produce compassion in Joseph. It was also calling for compassion to cause mercy to effect justice or the justice system of the land. Read Genesis 45:1-9, which shows the effectiveness of Jacob's prayer of compassion or mercy-favor.

Type 2—Loving Kindness

This is a loving kindness where mercy is leadership, not abandoning what has been redeemed when people miss the mark.

We see this in Genesis 15:13: "In your lovingkindness You have led the people whom You have redeemed; in Your strength You have guided them to Your holy habitation."

This mercy-loving kindness was not only shown in not destroying Israel for sin, but it is the redeeming of those He chooses and the teaching and guiding of those chosen to reach maturity and their purpose in life. It's a guiding system that teaches people how to walk into their destiny.

It's not a matter of overlooking an error in judgment or choices. It is having a hand to guide you through the valley of the shadow of death, so that you emerge victorious on the other side.

Type 3—Mercy-Judgment

This is a concept that can be understood from the Ark of the Covenant and the mercy seat that sat upon it. We read in Exodus 25:17-21 the godly concept of mercy and judgment: "And you shall make a mercy seat of pure gold, two and a half cubits long and one and a half cubits wide."

Pure gold is the pure undefiled righteousness of God. It also represents the true, unfailing love of God. Mercy carries a beauty with it that is holy and good, and it shines like gold in the presence of those loved. Pure gold signifies a warmth and acceptance. A two and one-half cubit length and a one and one-half cubit width represent the number four or door to heaven and mercy. The fourth commandment is a covenant commandment to release mercy on God's marked or called out peoples.

The dimension of the mercy seat calls for 1500 years from the Noachian flood until judgment is given over Egypt and sin, as well as the 2500 years from the punishment of Judah until the punishment of Israel in the lands given to Manasseh and Ephraim.

Verse 18: "And you shall make two cherubim of gold, make them of hammered work at the two ends of the mercy seat." Most people recognize these angels as Michael and Gabriel, archangels who are righteous and loyal to God. They are attached to the mercy seat, just as justice and discipline need to be tempered by mercy's compassion.

Verse 19: "And make one cherub at one end and one cherub at the other end; you shall make the cherubim of one piece with the mercy seat at its two ends." Remember these cherubs were to be hammered or tested and proven loyal to the mercy seat and Him who sat upon it. They needed to be part of it in order to show that mercy, justice, and discipline are functions of Jesus who sits upon the mercy seat.

Verse 20: "And the cherubim shall have their wings spread upward, covering the mercy seat with their wings and facing one another; the faces of the cherubim are to be turned toward the mercy seat." The spreading of the wings not only implies honor, but also forgiveness is functioning with mercy in directing justice and discipline. It also means to be attentive to the Word.

Verse 2: "You shall put the mercy seat on top of the ark, and in the ark you shall put the testimony which I shall give to you."

The ark carried the covenants, the Torah, and the bread of heaven. However, mercy was the ruler of them all. All judgment for breach of the law or covenants had to be dealt with in mercy before justice and discipline could act. People would be given a time to repent and confess their sins before the wages of sin could be extracted. A refusal to repent or acknowledge one's sin would result in justice claiming one's life. God is not mocked.

Type 4—Mercy is Covered in Atonement

The first law of atonement is found in Exodus 33:19: "And He said, I, Myself will make all my goodness pass before you, and will proclaim the name of the [Eternal] before you; and I will be gracious [merciful] to whom I will be gracious [merciful], and I will show compassion on whom I will show compassion."

We can ask for forgiveness, mercy and strength, but it is Jesus who must decide when and how mercy will be shown and flow.

The second law of atonement is found in Leviticus 16:2 "And the Eternal said to Moses, 'Tell your brother Aaron that he shall not enter at any time into the holy place inside the veil, before the mercy seat which is on the ark, or he will die, for I will appear in the cloud over the mercy seat.'"

Atonement-mercy calls for a covering of sin for a nation. It calls on Jesus to deal in peace for the nation of believers. And if you attempt to approach the throne of God without blood, you will die, for you must be sin free at that time.

The third law of atonement is found in Leviticus 16:13 "He shall put incense on the fire…"

The incense represents the prayers of the nation of believers. It represents also the acknowledgment of breaches to the covenants and laws, including using human strength in keeping the words of God without the grace of God. The mercy seat is calling upon Jesus to bear and endure the efforts of man to obey, to love, and to prosper while walking in his own strength.

Leviticus 16: 14 "Moreover, he shall take some of the blood of the bull and sprinkle it with his finger on the mercy seat and on the east side; also in front of the mercy seat he shall sprinkle some of the blood with his finger seven times."

The bull's blood represents the priesthood and the seven eras of churches of God that would come after the death of Jesus. It represents the seven churches, and the seven types of priests, pastors, teachers, apostles, ministers, prophets and evangelists who would guide Jesus' churches through those ages. They would all need access to the mercy seat and the life-giving spirit of Jesus.

Atonement mercy was again shown in Leviticus 16:15 "Then he shall slaughter the goat of the sin offering which is for the people, and bring its blood inside the veil and do with its blood as he did with the blood of the bull, and sprinkle it on the mercy seat and in front of the mercy seat."

The High Priest sacrificed the goat so the people could come for mercy. However, only the Priest could bring the blood of the goat and sprinkle it. This atonement mercy did several things:

1. It allowed Jesus to present His own blood.
2. It gave mankind access to call on the blood to change them.
3. It gave mankind permission to be washed clean by the blood.
4. Mankind as believers could use the blood as a weapon.
5. Poisons, toxins, and disease could now be washed clean.
6. Requests before the Father could be made through the blood.
7. Renewal and confirmation of promises and covenants could occur.

When we acknowledge the sprinkling of the blood upon the mercy seat, we can call upon all the mercy of Jesus who sits upon it. It becomes our job to grasp the value of the mercy of God. As we receive, so must we give or our supply is cut off.

Type 5—Mercy by Intercession.

To understand this we must see Moses' prayer in Numbers 14:18-19 'The [Eternal] is slow to anger and abundant in lovingkindness [mercy], forgiving iniquity and transgressions; but He will by no means clear the guilty; [allowing the] visiting of the iniquity of the fathers on the children to the third and fourth generations.' "Pardon, I pray the iniquity of this people according to the greatness of Your lovingkindness [mercy], just as You also have forgiven this people, from Egypt even until now."

The people were not yet willing to seek forgiveness for their love of sin. Moses interceded for the twelve tribes of Israel. He called on the mercy of Jesus to forgive or pardon their iniquity even though he declared that they needed judgment.

Look how Jesus responded: "I have pardoned them according to your word; but indeed, as I live, all the earth will be filled with the glory of the [Eternal]" (Numb. 14:20-21).

Calling on the mercy of God not to destroy the twelve tribes of Israel resulted in a release of the glory of God. Jesus wouldn't let all of Israel be destroyed, just those twenty-one and over who had seen His miracles and refused to come out of murmuring, grumbling, and complaining. A forty-year penalty was imposed for the fathers to die off. The mercy in intercession caused a reduced judgment.

Type 6—Mercy in Blessing

Deuteronomy 7:9 says: "Know therefore that the [Eternal] your God, He is God, the faithful God, who keeps His covenant and His lovingkindness [mercy] to a thousandth generations with those who love Him and keep His commandments."

Jesus seeks to bless, and He is faithful to those who keep His covenants and His commandments out of love. Moses called us to know Jesus as the Faithful God. To receive Jesus, the Faithful and the Merciful, we need to be prepared to love Him.

His mercies are for us, and they are new every morning. The loving kindness of God is not released out of duty to obey but out of love. Receiving mercy means the receiving of freedom and happiness.

Type 7—Revelation

To begin to understand this mercy, we need to examine 2 Samuel 7:12 "When your days are complete and you lie down with your fathers, I will raise up your descendants after you, who will come forth from you and I will establish his kingdom."

This is a mercy or loving kindness to know that David's descendants would sit upon the throne.

"He shall build a house [temple] for My Name, and I will establish the throne of his kingdom forever" (2 Sam. 7:13). This revelation let David know that Solomon's bloodline would establish the coming Messiah and bring the Kingdom of God that could never be destroyed. And from his line there would be kings to sit upon the throne of many nations.

Verse 14 reveals that out of encouragement, David would know that Jesus would never leave his family no matter what his children did until the end of the age. No others could ever be chosen to replace David's children.

Verse 15 guarantees God's mercy to David. This mercy is not only revelation but also a double blessing in encouragement. Jesus spoke the mercy in two different formats, thus closing the possibility of change from the east or west or from infinity to infinity.

Mercy involves more than even these seven basic types. Research it and know the love and heart of Jesus as He gives judgment in this age from the mercy seat.

I pray peace into your soul, enabling the mercy of God to fill your soul so that confidence will release the grace to change and grow in Jesus.

CHAPTER 12

Bored With Jesus?

T he world has turned sour to hearing the words of Jesus, His name, His teaching and His good news that He came to give us. Have you joined the world's rejection of truth and become bored with Jesus? Have you joined the walking dead who don't know Jesus or His message of love, hope, and purpose?

Jesus came to give us the gospel or good news that has become perverted over the years. Christians and believers have either never heard the good news or never bothered to study into its true meaning, which is why the false gospel of no-law grace is acclaimed without examination. The good news or gospel is the Kingdom of God, explained in *Hidden Truth from Prophecy—Beyond 2012*.

However, the world is expecting bad news, not good news. They are interested in feeding on the bad news, but they are bored with the good news of God's Kingdom coming to earth. Are you? If so, why? Here's how to find out. We relate here our apostle's sermon on this subject.

Question # 1: "So why have you *lost your first love?*"

The answer is not an orderly decline or an orderly procedure. Loss requires a number of open doors. The word in Hebrew is *chata*, whose root meaning is to miss, as well as all these definitions:

- To choose sin as to abort the harvest or blessings of God.
- To forfeit a close relationship, possession, wage, or increase.
- To create lack in one's life.
- To expect a yoke, bond, tie, or attachment.
- The report of a vow, contract, or bond.
- To lead one astray.
- To condemn, thus ending a relationship, or communion.
- To no longer rely upon, or have for enjoyment.
- To do harm to a relationship, partnership or marriage.
- To employ or neglect to ensure loss.
- To miss or misplace.
- To create offense or be offended.
- To sin against.
- The act or condition of purging.
- The emptying of bad to accept good.
- To trespass on another's barriers, love, trust, or belief.
- It also means to establish a pathway for grief, dismay, despair, and/or disinterest.
- To attack and control one's life.

So we can see that *chata* is a loss that brings us to grief and into the yokes of sin consciousness. We avoid thinking of Jesus and having His Word to be on our tongues. Loss causes an inward, self-reinforcing program of erosion. The less you think on Jesus, the less you are able to do so.

If you never talk or listen to your mate, and never read your mate's words, you wander away from your mate and into the arms of another. This is the way that most people have lost their first love for Jesus. After you get bored with Jesus, you tend to never return to find Him.

Question # 2: "Why have you forgotten your identity?"

People want to see themselves as owning a problem, sickness, debt, hopelessness, loss, anger-rage or other sin. They even see themselves as owning the attacking demons. They readily claim false identities in Satan. Yet they refuse to make room for their identity in Jesus. Their heart is so filled with falseness that the concept of belonging to goodness, loving kindness, mercy, and forgiveness can't settle into their heart. When you cannot accept belonging to love, you forget quickly who you are chosen to be in Jesus.

Without an identity, your heart doesn't see life, health, prosperity, peace, and love as belonging to you. It is seed sown on stony ground that the birds or demons can quickly see and steal from you. You don't protect what your heart can't find room to accept. That's why people forget their *identity* so quickly when Satan moves to attack. We surrender the "who we are" and the authority that goes with it.

No identity will always mean that you will lose interest in following Jesus, learning what Jesus has to think or say, and lose authority to change facts as presented by Satan into the truth as spoken out by Jesus as the Word of life and truth.

Question # 3 "Why have you ignored your covenant commitments?"

Covenants are misunderstood. They aren't simply agreements, contracts, bonds, promises, or vows. The Hebrew *berith* means to cut cleanly in two so that as the conditions are declared, one walks through the blood and around each section of the animal creating a sideways eight or an infinity sign. This creates a blood vow with each loop through it— a confederacy, a marriage of families, a league of responsibilities and an eternal blood covenant that can't be broken except by the death of the covenant partner or his family. If one member of a covenant fails to keep his responsibilities, he must die.

The adding of additional covenants doesn't end the power, authority or the responsibility of the previous covenants. It can only add to or change a conditional term and spell out new responsibilities. This added covenant could also add new families to agree with the covenant.

In the Second Testament, the ninth covenant was sealed in the body and blood of Jesus through the communion service. It manifests all prior covenants between God and man. It is to be a covenant reminder of our responsibilities in a daily refresher or reminder that we have a supreme covenant in Jesus.

Yet many haven't recognized their responsibilities that they committed to each time they take the communion service. Some even think that the reminder is only to be repeated once a year at Passover.

As Satan gets you to forget to have communion and to review your responsibilities, he gets you bored with seeking more of Jesus. This authorizes Satan to steal from you, destroy opportunities, lie to you, and most of all kill you for breaking a covenant.

Question # 4 "Why have you abandoned the truth?"

Jesus is the Word and the Speaker of the Word for both biblical testaments. His Word is truth in both testaments. He teaches the second by quoting the first. If the foundation doesn't stand, neither does the rest of the building, in this case, the Second or New Testament. The fact that the second relies on the first is proof that the second has truth and authority behind it.

When theologians attempt to discount any part of truth, they create a deception and a lie that twists truth so that good and bad are established as an understanding. They attempt to change who God is and what He thinks and speaks. This confuses the believers so as to find contradictions with God. *Trying to sort out truth becomes a burden.* They seek the easy road and believe the theologians since they can see them. The result is them becoming bored with Jesus.

Question # 5: "Becoming angry with Jesus?"

Jesus doesn't fight fair. He doesn't explain Himself and He doesn't justify Himself. If you can't argue with Jesus as to why He allows disasters, why someone was allowed to die, why someone was born deformed, or even why He didn't strike that so and so down who cut you off in traffic, then why study Jesus?

How do you maintain interest in a Being who secludes Himself in the clouds of heaven? How do you hear His name or His words spoken or know His thoughts or His love while you reside in the turmoil of anger? You can't; therefore, it's easy to get bored with Jesus.

Question # 6: "Why have you become so compromising with the Word?"

People love to hear the truth about others, but they always alter the facts about themselves. They manipulate the truth in order to explain, justify, and redeem themselves. When people compromise the Word, they rely on works of the flesh to make them righteous. And the Word keeps reminding them that dead works don't give life. Jesus is life, His works are living, and it is His blood that washes us clean. Jesus gives us His grace or empowerment and His righteousness. He becomes the Divine Master of our lives.

When people compromise the Word, they try to make Jesus obey their personal standards and become a god made in their own image. Pride steps in and our self-righteousness says that we don't need Jesus or His wisdom. Whoever is first priority in our life becomes god, and we become bored with Jesus and abandon all truth for the love of a lie.

Question # 7: "Why does your faith falter at the first signs of adversity?"

Here lies a deceptive understanding of balance. When everything is going well, who needs Jesus? When prosperity flows, who needs to be taught by the Word? Satan will lull people to sleep so they become bored with Jesus, His Word, and His revealed knowledge. The more bitter the times, the more intense our relationship with Jesus needs to be.

When you are lulled into an unbalanced situation, you seek fear rather than love to bring balance. Your faith falters when it should be strong because you have trusted in things and not Jesus. Luxury, wealth, or status is what you were seeking; therefore, in a time of trouble, there is *no* strength to produce the faith needed to defeat the adversary. And when you are bored with Jesus in favor of good times, the false gods eat you alive.

Question # 8: "What have you done with the grace that the Father has given you."

The empowerment of any grace is Jesus and thankfulness for that grace. You may be empowered to succeed at something, but laziness, squandering, and bitterness will prevent you from working with the available grace. When you are bored with Jesus, you don't claim that grace, and you make no move to exercise it. How much new grace can you call on when you chose to abuse, neglect, or disown the empowerment already given to you?

Question # 9: "Where is your zeal?"

If you have no zeal for Jesus, you will have no love for Him to be part of your life. When you have no love for Jesus, then how often will you go out of your way to obey Him, to trust Him, or to seek Him out?

When there is no zeal to know Jesus, there is no intimacy, so no love develops and you quickly become excessively bored with Jesus, His Name, His teachings, and His promises.

You don't let the identity of Jesus join with your heart or will when zeal is missing. You will rely on the process of "overthink" to undermine everything Jesus has for you.

Question # 10 "Where is your hope when you get bored with Jesus?"

Without hope, we will refuse to claim:

- Forgiveness
- Peace
- Prosperity
- Protection
- Health
- Joy
- Life
- Strength
- Redemption
- Renewal
- Release
- Freedom
- The Rapture
- Rewards
- The Graces
- Partnership
- And the Eternal Love

When hope is lost, identity is open to theft or twisting, and boredom comes. Your hope and calling are brushed aside in favor of fear or things.

When boredom reigns in your life, you declare yourself a sinner, a wretched person, a loser, and/or a failure, and Jesus has no home or temple in your spirit man. Disbelief, disinterest, apathy and rebellion invade you.

I pray that you will turn over to Jesus all areas where boredom has touched you and that your zeal and love for Jesus will bring you out of the pit of despair caused by boredom. You will then be able to turn your heart to the Father.

CHAPTER 13

The New Moon Breakthrough—
Turning Over the Past to Jesus

W hy haven't God's children been able to turn their hearts to their Father in heaven? The reasons are multiple, but one stands out: they have too much baggage. They carry around a past of guilt and shame that they haven't been able to turn over to Jesus. Some have taken the important first step of burying their old man and the old ways in baptism. But most have no idea or understanding about an important end-time revelation that completes the process.

We're speaking of the laying down of long-term pains and problems to Jesus on the new moon, when the moon is completely darkened. All mankind will one day bow down before Jesus at the new moon and as they enter the Sabbath day, surrendering their burdens to the Burden bearer (Isa. 66:23; 1 Pet. 5:7; Mat. 11:28-30; 2 Chron. 2:4). Our book, *God's Fruit of Forgiveness*, discusses the subject in detail, and especially our e-book, *New Moons—New Lives*.

Many on Freedom Blog have enthusiastically expressed the release and freedom they received as they begin to practice this new moon understanding. We are spirit beings who have souls (minds, hearts or emotions, and wills) and live in bodies. Laying down long-term problems at the new moon has allowed these people to take dominion over their souls. The releasing of the soul's residue of the past to Jesus has allowed their souls to be filled up with more of Him.

Fear of Loss

Job's words and actions prophesied one of the main burdens believers would need to lay down to Jesus in the last days: the fear of loss.

Job feared the loss of his children (Job 1:5; 3:25), and what he feared came upon him. Satan thought erroneously that if God withdrew His blessings from Job that he would curse God and die (Job 1:11), as his wife encouraged him to do. But Job stayed steadfast, and although he sought answers from God, he never cursed Him (Job 42:8). His faithfulness under trial paves the way for us in this end time to pass our tests and give all fear of loss to Jesus, which is always more difficult in a society that has made wealth and pleasure its god.

Let's be honest with God and ourselves. What fears of loss do we entertain? Which one of these items are we afraid of losing: life, mate, family, pleasures, respect, weaknesses, addictions, house, wealth, selfishness, youth, pride, job, business, peace, ease, hair, beauty, understanding, sicknesses, strength, or health?

Fears give Satan a right to attack since we are inviting in one of his principle demons. Even our Christian friends can cause us to sow the seeds of the fear of loss. Peter tried to get Jesus to fear the loss of the life He knew He had to give for mankind (Mat. 16:22-23). In the original language Jesus basically said to Peter, "Satan is using you to try to block my vision and purpose."

Jesus tells us to deny ourselves, turning over our fears of loss, taking up our cross or purpose in life in order to pass the test of the fear of loss (Mat. 16:24-26). Everything that we put ahead of Jesus will be lost, but everything we turn over to Him that binds us to the fear of loss will be saved. What fear of loss are we willing to turn over in order to profit fully from the abundant, eternal life Jesus offers us?

What fear of loss can Satan employ to cause us to curse God? Where are we willing to hide from the face of God to avoid dealing with our fears of loss? Here are some places we might be hiding: drugs, alcohol, sugar products, music and loud noise, sex, sleep, diets, philosophy, religiosity, anger, legalism, stupidity, ignorance, "workaholism," boastfulness, TV, books, gossip, fault finding, unforgiveness, rituals, debt, politics, and cursing others.

Normally we choose several hiding places, but all fears of loss are gifts of Satan, as are our efforts to cover them up with excuses. We need to lay down both to Jesus at the new moon.

New Moon Questions and Comments

Here are some questions and comments bloggers at Freedom Blog have posted…

One man asked if it's best to lay things down at the church altar or in our home? His neighbor has an altar in her home, and he asked if this altar could this one be used?

"… if the church is a Sabbath keeping church, that would be a good idea. The highest level of anointing would be in a Sabbath keeping, new moon keeping church. We wouldn't recommend it for a Sunday keeping church, nor would we recommend the neighbor's altar unless they also use it for the new moon. Your personal altar would be preferable. That could be your normal place of prayer or a table you designate for that purpose."

A local man told us that on the last new moon he turned over his son whom he had not seen in twelve years. He didn't know if he was dead or alive. He had been praying to God to bring him home or even get him to phone. Nothing ever happened. He turned him over and two days later he phones and says he is coming to Edmonton and wants to see his father. He was overjoyed beyond words to say.

He added that he and his son had a great reunion. They even prayed together and will be in regular contact from now on. He said that the power of forgiveness and the turn over sure tells us we have an awesome God.

Our youth leader in a neighboring city wrote that on a Sabbath new moon his group was looking at areas in their lives where they had been seduced into accepting ideas, concepts, traditions and beliefs that were set in place to bring them under the control of the New World Order. Their services lasted nearly ten hours. They were so engrossed in the Word and prayer that they had forgotten they were hungry. The Holy Spirit was fully present and Father Love blessed them with special understanding of freedom.

One of our most inspired bloggers related that the rains were so heavy last week that their basement got flooded with over a meter of water. On the new moon, her husband and she turned over all the fears of loss, damage, and contamination of the basement. Even though water flowed up to their door, the water began to recede Sunday in the basement. The next morning there was no water in the basement, no dampness, nor any mold or contamination. She could never have achieved this with all the spells that she had known in the works of darkness before her conversion. The power of turnover is proof that we have a God with whom nothing is impossible, when we trust Him.

One young lady related that she and her boyfriend left a certain church and joined a Sabbath home Bible study group. They were accepted and shown love immediately. They had read about this new moon, so they turned their old church and the problems it created over to Jesus on the new moon. They also asked Jesus to lead them to a place where He wanted them to be. They had gone out for lunch and were driving around singing praises when her boyfriend stopped and pointed to a house and said that is where Jesus wanted them to be. They went to the door and were immediately invited in to join in their Sabbath Bible study. She felt so blessed for turning over her last church.

One young man never believed that anything could ever help him deal with all the unforgiveness he was carrying to his dad and mom. He had read about myself in the [C-S Condition] and it made things seem even more hopeless. When he decided to try the new moon lay down, he kept hearing voices saying that this will never work. He ignored the voices and turned all the pain and unforgiveness over to Jesus. He spent Saturday in thanksgiving that he didn't have to carry the burdens. There was peace and joy in his heart when he awoke. He could even talk with a civil tongue to his parents. He now looked forward to the next new moon. He thanked us for explaining this doorway to peace.

One young lady had gone through the new moon taking all the things that she did while on drugs and turned them over to Jesus. She figured she should get rid of the shame and guilt that went along with it. She hoped she hadn't overstepped her bounds, but she sure felt good about downloading the works. She felt new and fresh, like getting a new start.

One man from India turned over all the pollution and misdirection from the sky lords over himself and his family. His grandparents, parents, brothers, sisters, and two uncles all showed up with the most amazing stories. They said that the day before they all felt like heavy pots were taken off of their heads. They all had dreams that he was somehow responsible and that they had to come to his home that morning. After he explained what he had done, they all left praising Jesus and the Father. They were saying that Jesus is truly the son of the Eternal God. They are also going to look into the keeping of the Sabbath. He exclaimed that God is wonderful.

One man decided to turn his wife and her unforgiveness, anger-rage, and a bunch of other things over to Jesus. His wife decided to seek out help in dealing with her problems. She even apologized for the evil ways that she had been treating him. The more she read and understood information from our site, the more certain she was that God's hand was upon us.

One Jewish gentleman checked with the Rabbi to see if our celebration of the new moon was correct and if it had sufficient proof. He said it was a time of taking ones cares, doubts, sins, and heartaches to the altar and turning them over to the Eternal. He had said that its greatest use was during the time of King David. But it quickly fell out of favor with all the other kings. He asked how we found out about it since the Rabbi said Jews never talk about it or publish on it?

We answered, *Thanks for that info. Our understanding is that it was revelation given to our apostle. He was curious as to why the Bible spoke so often about the new moons. We have previously simply understood that they were markers to know when to keep the feasts (with the exception of the new moon of Trumpets.) We began its observance in much of the present way just before Pentecost four years ago. We began keeping it, and as we obeyed, more revelation came.*

One young man was no longer seeing himself as a victim who needs to stay in unforgiveness and run for vendetta. When he turned all the pain to Jesus, turned over the unforgiveness, he wrote in all caps, "WHAT A SENSE OF FREEDOM!"

One young lady kept hearing voices in her head that God didn't love her because she hadn't suffered enough to please Him. The voices shouted in her head that Jesus wouldn't' accept anything that she was going to lay down. She asked if God didn't love her and didn't want to hear her.

We have prayed for you, that you may have God's discernment and a realization of His great love for you. Those voices are not from God. He wants you to know that He loves you dearly, more than you can understand. Suffering does not please Him. Jesus suffered for you the penalty of sin. Penance is a demonic idea from the universal church, a terrible doctrine of demons. Give that falseness to Jesus on the new moon. Jesus does indeed want you to lay down your burdens, doubts, and fears. He will accept all you have to give Him. He paid dearly for all those pains that Satan has given you. Don't listen to those demons that are talking in your head. Tell them, "Satan and the demons, the blood of Jesus is against you!" God does not have it in for you. He has every good thing and every good and perfect gift reserved for you for the asking. Jesus wants to hear from you. Pour out your heart to Jesus at this new moon. Lay down all the darkness at this time of darkness, including the voices of darkness lying to you. Our Father is Love, and He loves you. Why else would you have connected with us?

She thanked us for our prayers and encouragement. She laid down the voices in her head, and never heard a single demon voice in her head. She felt good so she just kept praising Jesus all day long for her freedom.

A young lady and her boyfriend were planning to wed on a new moon but her aunt refused to attend because she said that any marriage that takes place on the new moon is cursed by God and will bring nothing but bad luck. She asked about this.

Jesus married Adam and Eve on the eve of a new moon, the Day of Trumpets, the Bible indicates. There is no command not to marry on certain days, and certainly not the day of the new moon. What you must do is reject and break off the authoritative curses from your aunt with communion, and it would be wise to break off witchcraft curses since her activities seem suspect. God is not cursing you, but she is, and there is only bad luck for one who accepts it. We don't live by luck but by blessings.

They got married on the new moon and the honeymoon was great. Her aunt relented and came to the wedding. She apologized for her negativity and cursing. She gave them the down payment for a new house. She felt God was wonderful.

CHAPTER 14

Are You Religious -- or for Real?

Religilous, the recent movie that poked irreverent fun at religion is a sign of the times. God said mockers would be plentiful and loud in these last days. Sadly, mockers don't have to look hard to find hypocrisy and scandals in religion.

One of the greatest barriers to God's children turning their hearts back to their Father in heaven is the dangerous and prevalent spirit of religiosity. Religiosity isn't a friend to the one who wants to know God the Father and His love. Religiosity is an enemy of love. It's a demon!

While sitting in the same place in church as a habit is not always a bad thing, in some churches the pew is part of the church routine and can be, as the Pharisees who sat in the chief seats, an aspect of religiosity. And when you make the play on words and take another word pronounced "pew," you can describe what God thinks of man's attempt to worship Him -- or religion. Simply put, it stinks. As the French would say of rotten eggs, "Ca pu!"

Religiosity stinks to high heaven! God detests it.

But what is it? The dictionary says: "a set of *beliefs* concerning the cause, nature, and purpose of the universe, esp. when considered as the creation of a superhuman agency or agencies, usually involving *devotional and ritual observances*, and often containing a moral code governing the conduct of human affairs."

While God does speak of true religion in His Word, human religion started with Cain. It's basically this in resume form: "We will worship

You, God, the way *we* decide, and You'll just have to like it or lump it. We choose to base our beliefs and rituals on *man's* ideas and traditions, on the opinion of human beings led by demons." Doesn't sound too good, does it? But stripped of the niceties, of which religion is full, that is what human religion is.

The modern Hebrew word for religion is *dat*, daleth tav, or the door to the sign or cross. It is based on one of the biblical words for law or decree. True religion is based on the law or Word of God. True religion based on God's Word is indeed a door to the cross of Jesus. It is based on Jesus, His blood, His name, and His Word.

Religiosity is the antithesis of true religion. This spirit has a hold on our Western churches especially, and it holds us back from turning the hearts of God's people back to Him in true love and worship. How can you worship God in spirit and truth when a demon is dictating how you worship?

We recently were taken aback by a situation in which we were asked to pray. A grandmother called our apostle to explain a strange situation in a Protestant church in the Northeastern U.S. Her husband had passed away, and the service was taking place in their church. Her grandson of eight years had not seen his grandfather since his passing, and he wanted to see him again.

This youngster had learned in Sunday school about Jesus raising the dead. And unlike most adult Christians who think they can't do that because that was Jesus, and He was special, this young boy actually believed what he had learned. And he acted on it!

He ran to his granddad's open casket and jumped in, calling on Jesus to raise him up! And He did! The grandfather rose out of his casket to the stupefaction of the onlookers.

We would be tempted to call their reaction "stupidfaction" when you hear what they did. The pastor and others condemned grandfather and grandson with being witches and warlocks and kicked the whole family out of the church. The church persecuted them so cruelly that they had to move to another state!

With religious friends like that, who needs enemies! They see a wonderful miracle before their eyes, and they can't believe Jesus in that boy could do such amazing things. It must have been witchcraft. "Father, forgive them. They don't know what they're doing." That's what we counseled this woman to say.

What a blatant example of the ridiculousness of our "religulous" churches!

The Religious Churchgoer versus the True Believer

Many demons work with the spirit of religiosity. Two of the main ones are legalism and stinginess. We will look at those a bit later, but first we shall contrast the religious person and the true believer, or religiosity and true Christianity.

We like to define religiosity as man's attempt to worship God as *he* (man) sees fit or even more revealing: man's attempt to show God how good he is, how good *he* (man) is, showing God what to do, making God in His own image. It's all about giving God a makeover. Do you ever get mixed up and think you're the Potter and God's the clay? It doesn't work that way!

Religiosity includes:

- Tradition.
- Lord worship and pagan holidays, Sabbath-breaking.
- Trying to make God in your own image.
- Thinking you can manipulate God.
- Vain, repetitious prayers.
- Routines.
- A form of godliness that denies its power.

We need to understand religiosity because it is a frequent enemy. In addition, it has affected most of us to some degree, and it is part of our church anointing in Isaiah 58. We are called to restore the Sabbath. We are also called to raise our voice like a trumpet and declare to God's people their transgression and to the house of Jacob their sins.

Robert B. Scott

Who is Jacob? Jacob represents the unbelievers, all of them in the world, even those who believe they are believers but aren't. Many churchgoers don't know Jesus, and that can include some prominent churchgoers such as pastors. As some have said, standing in a garage doesn't make you a car, and sitting in a church doesn't make you a believer in Jesus.

We heard the story once of a man who woke up one Sunday morning and didn't want to go to church. His mother chided him, only to hear numerous excuses. Finally, he asked his mother to give him three good reasons why he should go to church. She said, "Well, first of all, it will help you to be a better person. Second, it's Easter Sunday. And third, you're the pastor!"

Our Anointing

We are called to declare to the nation and even the unbelievers their sins and come against religiosity, which permeates the religion of believers and non-believing churchgoers alike. Isaiah 58:2 says, "Yet they seek me day by day…" Many in the universal church have daily mass, and God calls it what the French call it: "la messe"— a mess! It's a tangled, empty web of ritual that keeps us far from our Father Love. His heart yearns for us to turn to Him and His love, but religiosity is the antithesis of love.

The New International Version continues in Isaiah 58:2: "… they *seem* eager to know my ways [religiosity puts on a front of role playing; religious people *play* religion], *as if* they were a nation that does what is right." Eighty per cent of Americans say they are Christian! Canadians are less pretentious. Betrayal attacks the Canadian churches whereas religiosity has a hold on the American churches.

Jesus' words give us a case study in religiosity—those famous Pharisees. In Matthew 23:2-7, Jesus said to do what they said, not what they did. They poured burdens on others they wouldn't dare carry themselves. They did all their deeds to be noticed by men.

Pharisees do everything to be seen as holy by God and others, but it's a farce. Second Timothy 3 in context describes *church people* in the end time. Selfishness and love of pleasure isn't limited to non-believers.

Timothy says they would have a *form* of godliness, while denying the power thereof. He talks of these last days as difficult times where "men will be lovers of self, lovers of money…" What most people don't see here is the punch line in verse 5 that bears repeating, "holding to a *form* of godliness, although they have denied the power."

These are professing Christians! These are Christians who are "lovers of pleasure rather than lovers of God." And maybe it's no coincidence that Paul said the culprits would be men. They don't have a corner on selfish behavior, but God did tell them to love their wives for a reason. He didn't need to tell women to love their husbands.

The power of a true believer is in the power of love. True godliness packs great power, but we don't see Christians walking in power and authority. They exchanged the mighty name of Jesus for the limp lord, a weak wimp of a demon named quagmire or the man/god with the stupid, unprintable name referring to a man's sexual organ replacing his brain. He's also called Baal, who thought and ruled through his penis rather than his head, loving pleasure more than God.

Timothy says, "Avoid such men!" Obviously, he wasn't talking about people in the world. He said not to fellowship with those who had a form of godliness—in other words, not to fellowship with those who love only "the Lord" and not Jesus! Now we realize that at this writing many sincere Christians love Jesus but have never learned the origin of the word Lord, saying it because they don't realize it's a calculated mistranslation to rob believers of their power and intimacy with Jesus.

God doesn't judge them, but they are missing out on so much of Jesus. You don't have to miss out. We hope you're not offended by us calling Lord worship what it is in reality—calling our Savior by the name of a demon and a false god who was worshipped for the size of his sexual equipment.

God says to stay away from the fellowship of those who have a form of godliness, who worship the demon religiosity. They are busy doing their own thing and telling God He must approve. We are called intolerant if we don't join with them in their worship of the Lord and his companion religiosity. We are called, of course, to love all men, even Christians who have been deceived. God meets them in love and mercy where they are, and so should we.

Religious versus Real

We will now contrast religious versus real.
Religiosity involves the following:

- A form of godliness.
- Talking the talk only.
- Emphasizing the exterior versus true godliness.

Being real in Jesus means:

- A changed heart and mouth.
- Renouncing your own works for the righteousness of Jesus as a new creation.
- Walking the walk and talking the right talk, speaking out God's words, not Satan's.

Before we go any further, understand this: you must truly want to be real.

People don't like the book written by an apostle of the early church, who stood up and settled the issues of Acts 15. Some have called James an epistle of straw. No part of God's word is straw. It's all inspired. So listen to James: "If anyone thinks himself to be religious [in the true sense], and yet does not bridle his tongue but deceives his own heart, this man's religion is worthless" (James 1:26).

In Freedom Church of God we have been learning the importance of our words for fifteen years now, learning what to say and what not to say.

Because we are learning to be true believers, mature saints who are growing into perfection, and perfection is demonstrated by how we use the tongue, God is teaching us that our words have power!

"Pure and undefiled religion in the sight of our God and Father," says James, "is this: to visit orphans and widows in their distress, and to keep oneself unstained by the world." The obvious conclusion is that we see much impure religion today in the form of empty religiosity. We can see in 2 Timothy 3 that end-time religious people have allowed themselves to be overtaken and overly influenced by the wicked world around them. Pastors and evangelists beg for money. They are boastful: "My church is bigger than your church."

God calls them ungrateful, unholy. Quagmire pushes them from one ditch to the other, causing them to be destroyed for lack of knowledge. They are unloving (2 Tim. 3: 3) because, as we shall explore later, they see themselves as sinners that can't be loved by a holy God. They see themselves as unholy, and so they act in an unholy way.

Because of their feeling of inferiority, insecurity, and "unlovability," they have to judge, condemn, and talk about others and their faults to deflect attention from their own sins, becoming "malicious gossips."

They are "haters of good." God calls the Sabbath good, but they hate those who keep the Sabbath, the day of love. In so doing, they hate love. Paul is prophesying a warning to avoid the trap of hypocritical religiosity, not only to those under him in that day but also to true believers in these last days. If we are still affected by this demon, we need to lay it down to Jesus on the new moon and in the time of freedom from falseness during the Days of Unleavened Bread.

Paul says in verse 13 that "evil men and impostors [frauds] will proceed from bad to worse, deceiving and being deceived." Religiosity is all about deception, twisting the truth, bringing the truth down to a comfortable level of conformity to the world. Jesus says, however, that we must be transformed by the renewing of our mind. And how is our mind renewed?

As Paul explains to Timothy in the next few verses, we are renewed and protected against this onslaught of worldly religiosity by the Word of God. In verse 15, Paul tells Timothy to stay founded in the "sacred writings [of the Hebrew Scriptures, the only ones available at the time], which are able to give you the wisdom that leads to salvation…" In other words, we must be entrenched in the whole Word of God to be a true believer, to be real in contrast to all the false religiosity around us.

Religiosity Defined

To avoid religiosity and to be real, we need to understand more fully what characterizes this spirit of religiosity. Here are a few of its characteristics:

- Doing works for pride and for work's sake; doing just to be doing rather than *being*, than knowing your identity in Jesus, and having your works come forth out of your realization of who you are in Jesus.
- Routine and rote versus worship from the heart. The woman at the well in John 4 was focused on the physical aspects of worship, her fathers having worshipped on a certain mountain. The Jews said you had to worship in Jerusalem (v. 20). Jesus said the woman didn't know who or what she was worshipping, and He gave a key as to what our worship should be based on when He said, "You worship what you do not know; we worship what we know, for salvation is of the Jews" (v. 22). The door to the cross is found in the Hebrew Scriptures. And unless our religion or form of worship is based on biblical roots, it isn't the true religion. Paul exhorted the Gentile believer to become "partaker with them [the Jews] of the rich root of the olive tree [the anointed Word and holy days God gave to the Hebrew people]" (Rom. 11:17). That is the only way we can worship God, the way Jesus said to do in John 4. He said that "true worshippers will worship the Father in spirit and truth…God is spirit, and those who worship Him must worship in spirit and truth" (v. 22-24). True worshippers allow the Holy Spirit and

the Word to guide their worship. Religious services are dead. The holy convocations of true believers are full of life and light.

- Religious people seek security in rituals; true believers find their security in Jesus.
- Religious people don't walk in *love*. They judge others harshly and compare themselves with others. True believers esteem others better than themselves, walking in love and blessing others.
- Religious people say you have to be basically perfect before you come to Jesus, or at least before you come to their church. True believers heed Jesus' words to come to Him to find rest and for Him to teach them so they can grow to be like their Father Love (Mat. 11:28-31; Mat. 5:48).
- Religious people need rules and manmade regulations they feel they must obey to be acceptable to God. True believers obey God's laws of love because they love Jesus, having His love in them that pours out to others.
- Religious people like to sound religious and holy, making a show of righteousness. Spiritual theatrics are common. True believers can be expressive, but they don't put on a show. Their religion is of the heart.
- Religious people delight in the favor they feel they receive from God because of their "sacrifices" and offerings, even though God in both First and New Testaments says He doesn't delight in sacrifices but in worship from the heart, which is what true believers do.
- Religious people see themselves as sinners, displaying a false humility. True believers confess their sins and get on with it. They know their righteousness is not their own.
- Religious people try to bribe God. "If You do this, I'll do that." They can't get it into their heart that God loves them, that He has a covenant with them and promises to be faithful. They say please, not thank You like Jesus always did.
- Religious people have to pay for their sins with penance, which is related to poverty. They feel they have to be poor to do

penance. And if you're in the universal church, you can even pre-pay for the sin you plan with indulgences.

- Religious people make God in their own image. They make Him weak so they can identify with Him. They make Him into a God who wants to be worshipped corporately on Sunday, when Jesus called Himself the Divine Master of the Sabbath.
- Religious people use rituals to appease God into forgiving them, since they don't feel worthy of forgiveness. They whine and beg God for forgiveness, as well as for the answers to their prayers.
- Religious people think God is watching them to catch them in sin. They confuse Satan and God. Satan is the one who tries to make us sin and then catch us doing it.
- Religious people crave deception; they want to be lied to. True believers are hungry and thirsty for truth and righteousness.

Real Believers Know God Loves Them—Really!

The words spoken by the friends of Job show another major aspect of religiosity. Religious people don't believe God *loves* them. As Job's friends thought God was punishing him for sin, religious people think God is a harsh, vengeful God who only teaches us by trials and suffering. But that's not God. He is Love. Many Christians worship the Lord, who is either a cruel man-god named Baal, or a cruel demon named quagmire, who pushes you into the ditch.

Elihu's word embodied the ideas of Protestant theology. He referred to those who say, "God will rout him, or thrust him away [*nadaph*], shove him asunder." God is seen as wrathful, and His pastors are seen as loving to disfellowship people, to kick them out of their churches, ostracizing them.

Hear Elihu's self-righteousness of which he accuses Job: "My words are from the uprightness of my heart" (Job 33:3). Religious people love to sound so "sppp-iritual." Their lips intone righteous-sounding, syrupy prayers to look good in front of people. They put on a show. Even some anointed preachers mix religiosity with their messages and thus water down the anointing. The organ has to dramatically play in the background so the speech sounds more spiritual. They have to breathe in noisily between phrases to sound like some religious mentor that taught them how to sound spiritual. God's anointing doesn't need showy demonstrations based in the flesh.

David was a man after God's own heart. He was real. He sinned. Yes, he fell down badly, but he got up. He wasn't for the outward show, even as he danced from his heart in praise to God. He knew something religious people don't know.

He spoke it out in Psalm 51:16-17: "For You do not delight in sacrifice." In other words, God doesn't make a big deal of ritual. Even in the Hebrew Scriptures where rituals abounded because of the need to teach a physical people about the consequences of sin, God said He didn't delight in the rituals. "You are not pleased with burnt offering. The sacrifices of God are a broken [or repentant, humble] spirit; A broken and contrite heart, O God, You will not despise" (Ps. 51:16-17). God looks on the heart (1Sam. 16:7).

True believers receive God's love for them into their hearts. They hunger and thirst for more of Jesus and His Word, not for the empty traditions of men.

Religious people are empty. True believers, those who hunger and thirst for truth and righteousness, avoid the road to emptiness. Jesus said in Mathew 5:6, "Blessed are those [the true believers who stand out above the religious crowd], who hunger and thirst for righteousness, for they shall be satisfied." They will be filled with all the fullness of God.

So are you religious, or are you for real— a true believer?

CHAPTER 15

What is a Dead Man?

When a soul has left a body, the body is dead. When the soul is in the body, the body is alive. So what then is a dead man? I share here what God inspired our apostle to preach.

The wages of sin is death. The soul that sins, it shall die. ...So what then is a dead man?

The word "man" does not simply refer to a physical body. Genesis 1:27 says, "And God created man in His own image, in the image of God, He created him, male and female He created them."

Mankind was created to be male and female as two joining, supportive sexes. Their bodies were designed to please, to express physical love to each other and support and respond to each other.

However, something else exists as seen in the first part of Genesis 1:26, where God made man in the image of God, in His likeness, to have dominion.

It is one thing to be shaped like God, and it is another to be created in God's likeness and another again to be given authority to rule over the rest of what was created on the earth. The creation of mankind established a new thing, an extraordinary happening, an awesome shift in the order of things. Mankind was created with spirit, soul, and given an authoritative, speaking body. As the body was made male and female for interaction, support, and uplifting the spirit in man, man also needs interaction with God Himself. Otherwise man is a dead man walking.

Everyone who isn't in regular contact with Jesus is a dead man. Everyone who doesn't regularly feed on Jesus as the Bread of Life is a dead man. Everyone who doesn't accept the blood of Jesus is a dead man.

Genesis 2:7 says, "Then the [Eternal Creator] God formed man of dust from the ground, and breathed into his nostrils the breath of life, and man became a living being [a soul]."

We must examine what life or the breath of life is in order to discover what was given to man. It is first the spirit of life, which has two parts, the spirit *of* man and the spirit *in* man.

The spirit *of* man gives free moral agency, the ability to choose, and the spark that keeps the soul and body moving.

The spirit *in* man allows…

- Access to God.
- All revelation to be given to man.
- Access for the Holy Spirit to teach.
- Access for the Holy Spirit to speak through/with man.
- Power to create the seed/egg for reproduction.
- Power to heal oneself.
- Power to carry glory.
- Power to learn.
- Basis for faith.
- Desire for love and for giving love.
- Ability to trust God.
- Ability to appreciate humor.
- Ability to appreciate beauty.
- Power to visualize, see visions, and to dream dreams.
- Power to grow in power, strength, and knowledge.
- Power to guide the soul, to set the will.
- Power to control the body by what we speak.

Into the soul, the breath of life released…

- A will of the soul to maintain a course of action.
- A heart for learning, emotions, perception, fellowship, empathy, compassion, blessing, protecting, respect, life, thankfulness, gratitude, hearing, and learning to discern.
- A mind for organizing, remembering, understanding, discernment, communication between the brain and heart, talents, solutions, vanity, and for ciphering of numbers.

The breath of life gave something else to the soul that requires the will, heart, and mind to all work together in harmony. As the soul sets its will to know God, and comes under the Father's will, eight developers were released so that mankind could enjoy the abundant life and the joy-filled life. It would bring peace to every area of one's life in accordance with the love of God developed by the heart and will that appear as obedience and connection to God.

The Eight Developers

1. *Ingenuity*—This is the ability to solve problems, analyze, and theorize a mathematical solution. It involves applying math theorems, not previously known in the solving of a specific problem. It involves conceptual thinking that goes beyond the logic and reasoning of the average thinker. It's very common among dedicated born again believers who obey the Word. It's knowing what to do at the right moment but with no prior foreknowledge of a coming need for that information. It's knowing what to do when you never knew that you knew the answer, procedure, or math involved.

2. *Creativity*— Some call this artistic talent, a force for change, or even professionalism. Creativity is a means of handling an old technique, problem, or procedure in a new, more efficient way for the benefit of mankind. It is the use of one's abilities to

open new ground or express concepts with a new, more vibrant approach. Suppose a person is a writer by trade or profession. If he uses only rewriting techniques, he may have rewriting talent but not creative talent. This creative talent means writing something original in such a way that everyone would want to quote him, imitate him, or even sing like he did. Creativity produces trendsetters.

3. *Inventiveness*—This is the ability to develop something new that benefits society as a whole. This constitutes a blessing from God. In the last two hundred years, 326 inventions have met this condition. Three hundred and eight came from the US and Canada. Eighteen came from the rest of the world, nine came from South Africa and the United Kingdom, and two from New Zealand. The last invention in Canada, United States, South Africa, United Kingdom and New Zealand was made in 1971. All invention stopped after 1974 when the commandments, the Bibles, and the name of Jesus were removed from governments, schools, hospitals and the Armed Forces. Since 1972, 406 devices of destruction have been registered and put in use. Many have died, the power of invention has ceased, and the worship of the living God has also dropped to thirty-one per cent of the western world. There is a powerful correlation. The Anglo-Saxon peoples are God's chosen people of Israel, a people He blessed with the ability to preach the true gospel to the world. Their failure to do so and their rejection of the Creator who gave them their creativity has caused it to cease.

4. *Vision*— Vision does not only mean to visualize where you are at this moment in time. It also means:
   • To perceive a goal in life.
   • To perceive a path to a goal.
   • To see past the moment, problem, or set back.
   • To see the steps needed for success or victory.
   • To imagine one has the victory even before starting the course.

- To see an enemy and his weakness encountering the coming hand of God.
- To see God's love at work in your life, family, and nation.
- To see a room decorated before it is even furnished.
- To perceive a lesson, event, or statement from history.
- To perceive a location outside of time and space.
- To perceive a location for miraculous translation.
- To perceive ways and means of loving, joy, blessing, and meeting the needs in another's life.

It is with this lack of vision that people perish. Often people only see their problems, debts, sicknesses, and lack but can't see their solutions; they are therefore dead men.

5. *Motivation*—People who are alive are easily motivated to carry out right actions, judgments, and considerations. They are quickly back on their feet after they stumble or are pushed back by Satan. They see the enemy as defeated, and they are quick to get their hand back into the hand of God. To be motivated is to move hand in hand with God—to move with belief, trust, and love that God will never leave you or forsake you. Motivation is like going to a park where bullies have accosted you. But this time, your dad is going with you to ensure that you have fun at the park. Your motivation to play and have fun jumps up dramatically. You have security that moves you to action.

6. *Curiosity*—Curiosity is the ability to seek answers, to seek to learn, and to seek knowledge, understanding, wisdom, and discernment. It is like a newly walking child who wants to explore and know about everything. However, the focus has changed from things to God. We have tested the love of Father God, found it bigger than ourselves, our mistakes, and our sins, and we thus put our heart into knowing Him and His judgments, changing our values to be His.

7. *Inquisitiveness*—Inquisitiveness is a need to know the truth, especially about the things of God. Scientists place high

priority on knowing the truth about what God has created. Inquisitiveness is always related to knowing the truth about God, not things. It implies finding out how to use what becomes known of God in order to make everyone's life better. The inquisitiveness of scientists involves procedures and theorems. They theorize or guess at the solution, in actuality seeking to rise to the God level of knowledge— how God made things and how He keeps them working. Sadly, they sometimes fail to see God in everything created, thus losing or dulling ingenuity, creativity, and inventiveness.

8. *Purpose*—Purpose is a force of identity. It lets you know why you were born, where you came from, where you are, where you are going, what you are to do, and how to do it for the best results. Purpose is a gift from God and becomes employed as one learns to obey God. The purpose of a dead man is to accumulate money, protect wealth, and worry about losing it. The joys of life truly evade him and his understanding. He lives life in fear of everything even as he puts on a front. A person without purpose is plagued with emptiness and lacks the steadfastness to walk in integrity.

Have you passed these eight tests? Are you truly alive? Failing means you rely on death, fears, terrors and thrills to ensure and *feed the insecurity of anger-rage.* You become hostile, critical, condemning, and defiant until you breathe your last.

We have a choice as to whether or not we want to walk in life or walk as dead men (Deut. 30:19).

Have you cursed yourself with death? Here are some things you can say to do that:

- I am bored.
- Everything is so boring.
- I will just die of boredom.
- What's the use of living, everything always goes wrong.

Have you ever considered the root of the word "boring" or "boredom?" In ancient Egypt, the priests would drill holes through a person's skull in order to release headaches or remove tumors. Once a hole was drilled or bored, brain injury often occurred. When the Romans arrived in Egypt, they labeled this procedure, because of the lifeless existence these victims of the priests enjoyed. They were called dumb. The word bored-dumb was eventually contracted to boredom to refer to this practice.

To say, "I am bored," means I have allowed Satan to drill a hole and drain off all ingenuity, creativity, innovation, vision, and purpose for my life. I need someone to entertain me, therefore, because I can no longer think as a live person.

To say you will die of boredom means you have made yourself dumb by your choices and words. And unless you are entertained and emotionally stimulated, you will die; all fun, joy and happiness have left your life. You have also lost all motivation, curiosity, and inquisitiveness. Your body moves without soul life.

Jesus claims to be Life. And He came to give us life more abundantly. To move out of being a dead man, we need more and more of Jesus so that life may reside in us more abundantly.

Turn over to Jesus all claims you have made to wanting to be a dead man. Receive God's peace and *shalom* in your soul so that you will have nothing broken and nothing missing in living life as it should be lived.

Indeed, how can your heart turn to the Father's heart if you're a dead man? Come alive in Jesus, and turn your heart back to your loving Father. He's waiting to hug you and bless you as never before!

CHAPTER 16

Father of Lies or Father Love?

How can we turn our hearts to our Father of love and truth if we are holding the hand of the father of lies, Satan? We can't. It is extremely important that we understand how we have been conditioned by Satan to lie and accept lies. I thank my colleague Gerald Gudzinski once again for listening to God to receive this revelation.

Why are believers hesitant to speak out the Word of God?

Out of the abundance of the heart, the mouth speaks. Is the heart filled with the love of God's Word or filled with love for the devil's word? With what have you filled your heart?

Where did the desire to speak lies, the desire to twist and deceive come from?

They were birthed in Genesis 2: 16-17 where God forbade man from eating of the tree of the knowledge of good and evil.

Any time you mix good with evil, you get death. Any time you mix God's Word with Satan's word in your heart, you get heart problems, health problems, and mental problems. God has good reason to tell us not to eat from the table of God and the table of demons. Eating from the evil table will tear you apart, and you won't know what is killing you.

The basic root is just that: we don't want to know what is killing us. Bad words produce a bad tree that gives you bad fruit. Good words produce a good tree that gives you good fruit. When you mix the two, you always get poor results that bring lack, blockages of all good things and problems that are plentiful, more than you can deal with.

In Genesis 3:1 Satan in essence said, "Did God really say that you would die?" The words are rooted in planting doubt regarding the goodness of God. Doubt in His word and doubt in His provision and His judgment. Satan said to Eve, "Has that unfair God denied you access to every good tree for food in the garden?" People today say, "Oh yes, look at all the sins God doesn't want us to do." That's because they have gotten used to calling what is good evil and what is evil good.

The Hebrew here implies much had gone on before Satan closed the deal. Adam knew Satan was lying and allowed Eve to be deceived.

Deception from the Beginning

Is God the deceiver? People act like He is. Notice verse 3 where Eve answers Satan's question, "God has said, 'You shall not eat from it or touch it, or you will die.'" The Hebrew words reveal that it wasn't certain in her mind that this was going to happen. She was going out of her way to try to compromise with Satan so he was not so hostile and bitter. When you change the Word of God, you only do it to try to compromise with Satan.

The words Eve spoke opened the door for Satan to sow distrust, unbelief, and contention with God. Eve was prepared to contend with God after years of His provision in the garden.

Every time we don't speak out God's word into a situation, we are saying, "I am prepared to contend with God." But when we speak the Word of God out into a situation, we take mastery of the situation.

In verse 4 Satan told her she surely wouldn't die, in essence that God was pulling the wool over her eyes to control her and keep her a slave to ignorance. On the contrary, she accepted doubt and disbelief in the God who had shown nothing but love to her.

Satan established in her that she had the right to lie and live a lie. Satan likes to quote God's word but with a word added or subtracted so that it sounds similar, but is compromised.

In verse 5 he added a twist: "For God knows that in the day you eat from it your eyes will be opened, and you will be like God, knowing good and evil." What did he use as the justifier? To be like God, something he wanted. Satan wanted it and was telling them they didn't have it, but they did. He was after their power, so what he told them was that their ability to command or know things was being hindered.

Satan knew that neither Adam nor Eve had accepted their identity of who they were, what their destiny was, what their purpose was, and what power their words and choices released. They had been with God perhaps forty years, but they didn't allow it to connect.

Satan's Tactics

Satan takes this same route today to stop the children of God from doing the work as the sons of God. He steals their identity and power by convincing them to release their identity and power to him by misquoting God's word using complex justifiers, and we soak it in. For Satan to do this, he must...

- First cause us to compromise the Word.
- Cause doubt as to the validity of God's Word. "Well, it has never worked for me. God says He loves me, but He really doesn't. Remember that sin I committed that wiped me off the books with God?"
- Cause us to distrust God's good intentions and motives and His love for us.
- Cause us to disbelieve that God ever means what He says, that He is unfair, unfaithful, and is hiding good things from you.

When we understand Satan's base procedure, we see the root he uses to entice us into sin, lies, distrust, and unbelief in our God, actually conditioning us to lie.

How long have you been walking with God? Have you let anything connect? Have you let the Word of God connect with you, as to who you are?

When you walk with Him in His Word, you create the garden around you. It is our willingness to lie to God and to ourselves that is causing the problems. We've been conditioned to lie to ourselves and to God. We're told we can't succeed. God isn't going to honor our work.

Why not? We have dominion power on this earth; He has to honor His Word. So if we are speaking out His Word on the earth, He has to honor it. No matter what sin we have committed, He still has to honor His Word.

Our God, our Mighty God who cannot lie, who is love, knows good and evil. He is the one who defined it. God's choice is always good. Is your choice always good for you? Why not?

As soon as you are into dead works, you are into Satan's playing field. He's the master of death.

Isaiah 5:20 says, "Woe to those who call evil good, and good evil." We hear of devil's food cake and deviled eggs—small examples of how we call good evil. Today "wicked" means good.

Perversion of the Word

Look how many people take and pervert the Word of God. Why do you think we have so many denominations in the world? All of them have taken little bits of the Word and have perverted them—a little bit of truth and a lot of lies.

Satan is the father of lies. He wants you to believe a lie, to get involved in lying. If he can get you to compromise, twist the Word of God even slightly, he can use it against you. When we call evil good, then we take off the armor of God and the coat of righteousness that Jesus gave us in order to wear Satan's coat of sin. We aren't to be sinners; we aren't supposed to think sin. We're supposed to be thinking righteousness. But Satan says, "Taste this sin. See how pleasing it is for the moment. Don't judge it until you have tried it." You can only judge it after you become a slave to it.

Why are the Christians so willing to shun God? Have they not been born into conditioning? They see Him as a withholder of the things they think they have a right to experience. There are a number of reasons why people shun the tasting of God.

They don't have to meet with Him on the Sabbath Day. They've been taught that the Sabbath Day doesn't count. When you avoid meeting with Him on His appointed day, denying any visitation rights to God, of His mercy, and of His loving kindness, you will believe small lies that grow and grow.

They've commissioned Satan to stand guard over their hearts to pollute their minds and to bend their wills to his. They are conditioned to lie, holding their traditions above God's Word. They keep holidays rooted in paganism and seem to dare God to do anything about it. This is mocking God. It's a prideful refusal to be corrected. They want to hear what one of their friends has to say about what somebody else wrote about what somebody else wrote about what they thought God said, without ever reading the Word.

Isaiah 5:24 is a warning to those have "despised the word of the Holy One of Israel." Despised it, why? They have a love for evil and hate good. They don't trust God to live up to His word.

Isaiah 6:5 shows how Isaiah himself had allowed the lies around him to influence him. At the throne of truth and holiness, he saw how unclean his lips were and called himself "ruined."

The Defeat of Pride

The above word for ruined is *damah,* or perishing, which means to be dumb, silent, or speechless in the presence of God, to have failed to understand the power of God and His word, to cease making excuses and accusations against God, to be cut down to size in one's own eyes, to have one's pride cut off, to destroy all preconceived notions, to be brought to silence so that the power of sin has no power to act in one's life. It also means undone or rescinding all words one ever spoke that didn't line up with God's Word.

A better translation would be: "Woe is me for I am silenced, having been cut down in my pride, [not speaking the Word of God, but speaking from pride, the pride of lying], having failed to understand the reality, the power and the truth of God and His Word because I am a man of unclean, lying lips, and I live among people of unclean, lying lips."

Isaiah is saying that he is silenced from speaking his own words as he suddenly realizes that God is real and supreme, and that every word he has ever said that didn't line up with the Word of God was dross or death. He knew these words had to be undone or rescinded, or he was a dead man.

Lessons from Isaiah 6

We have said a lot of words over our lives that don't line up with God's Word, and we are dead men because of it. Isaiah understood in a moment that both he and all the nation of believers were conditioned to lie. Until he had admitted that everything that he had said was wrong, he was not allowed to see the face of God. From verse 5, we can learn this:

- Our pride teaches us to lie, to see God through a shield of lies and to speak out those lies.
- We are unclean in our lying. All the things we are doing are making us unclean.
- Speaking lies ruins us. Our life is cut down, cut short by speaking out lies, words of Satan that come from the tree of the knowledge of good and evil.
- A compromised word or phrase from God's Word is a lie. If you change the intent of God's word, you are speaking out a lie. You are saying you want to continue to eat from the tree of the knowledge of good and evil. God tells us prove all things and

only hold fast to the truth. Every excuse we use for not speaking God's Word is a love for lying.

- Every time we honor Satan by speaking his words, we mock and dishonor God.
- The Word of God disempowers the power of sin. When sin is trying to put a thought in your mind, speak out the Word of God. The thought that the power of sin was trying to implant is lost, neutralized.
- The Word of God cleans us up, renews us, and gives us purpose and life. When we don't speak the Word, we receive the opposite.
- We have the power to change, to repent of what we say or have said. We can acknowledge and rescind all wrong words.
- We can rescind and undo all past lies if we are willing to recognize them as lies and as sin, thus having a clean heart and clean lips established in us.

The Word of God tells us what we are to say and stand on. The lying words of Satan tell us what we are to fear, what we are to fail in, and what reason he has for killing us. So why does everyone want to speak Satan's words?

You have to want the truth, to want to see yourself as God sees you before you'll want a clean heart and clean lips. Ask God for this. Isaiah knew he had to ask for clean lips before God could give it to him. A person has to turn over to Jesus the unclean in order to receive the clean.

A seraphim took a burning coal from the altar and touched Isaiah's lips, and said his lips were clean and his sins forgiven. When a person is caught in the trap of lying, constantly speaking the words of Satan, it takes a miracle of Father God in order to overcome it. Recognize that you need a miracle, so God can work it in your life. One of the strongest sources of sin is lying. After he did this, Isaiah was able to go about speaking the truth and witnessing for God. You can too.

Signs of Inability to Speak the Word

Psalm 31:18 speaks of the liar in this amplified but faithful paraphrase: "The lips of the liar, deceiver, conniver, those who bear false witness against the righteous Word of God shall be mute (dumb, silenced and sealed). Those lips are filled with pride, contempt, and rejection of God." If you aren't willing to be trained by *every* word of God, then you aren't willing to be trained by *any* word from God. No picking and choosing.

A person who doesn't speak out the Word of God is:

1. Fearful and speaking out words of fear.
2. Too proud to trust God and His Word.
3. Showing contempt for Jesus and the Word that He is. Rejecting any part of the Word is rejecting Jesus, which includes the Sabbath day.
4. Rejecting everything God wants for them.
5. Has denied his identity in Jesus, thus making it hard to overcome sin.
6. Filled with words of defeat.
7. An advocate of doing penance and being judgmental.
8. A liar who will say anything to stay in lack, pain, loss, suffering, poverty, illness, and disability. They've already decided that they won't believe God but only what they see with their eyes. A liar doesn't want to sow the Word or have the seed watered with the Word, or have a harvest from the Word, thinking he can lie his way into heaven.
9. Prone to acknowledge Satan and be ungrateful to God for all His loving kindness. Satan has conditioned us to be ungrateful. We don't see how God is working with us and blessing us but are looking at the negative. You can only change the negative by speaking out the Word of God.

Psalm 52 shows us that God's loving kindness is continual and that we should meditate on the things of God and always be thankful. If we don't, like Eve we are willing to live in deception. David tells us to avoid evil speaking, unlike the world around us, especially in these last evil days. Wishing doesn't bring success; God's Word does.

Our willingness to seek out evil means that sin is rooted in your heart (Ps. 52:3). When we're ready to compromise the Word, we agree with Satan and open doors for Him. Ever hear or speak things like, "How is life treating you?" It means, "What sins have you done that you got away with or blamed others for doing?" When you ask a question, twisting it, you frame and build upon deceit. Our God wants our hearts and words pure and true to His Word so that we can be in the right alignment to be blessed.

In Psalm 51:9-10 David is asking for correction in his wrong speaking and the sins committed. Have we been asking Jesus to step in and clean our heart, change our heart, and alter what we speak? In verse 15 David wanted help in declaring from his heart the Word of God into every area of his life.

Have you been asking God into your life to change your weaknesses by His strength?

David wanted to use the words that God put into his mouth to praise Him; he not only wanted his whole language to be changed, but he also wanted to be able to praise God correctly. The willingness to turn over to Jesus all words, actions, and attitudes that are caused by lies and deception brings about a broken and contrite heart that is teachable and willing to hear what God has to say. Are you willing?

CHAPTER 17

The Unseen Enemy Destroying
Your Life and Marriage

What is the *real* cause of marital problems and most divorces? What is the *root* almost no one has discovered? Incompatibility? Unforgiveness? Financial disagreement? Wrong! It's a cloak you've probably never heard of—a cloak virtually unknown to marriage counselors. It's the *cloak of invisibility*. In the briefest of resumes, it's being ignored or taken for granted by your mate. Those who have the marital cloak over them usually start with the individual cloak, a real spiritual entity that has affected a vast amount of people — an entity ignored by those who counsel.

Do people ignore you? Do you feel they don't see or hear you? Do customers see other businesses and buy from them but don't see yours? Have you been overlooked? Have you spoken words that keep even God from seeing and hearing you? God gave us revelation on invisibility that blessed us all in our congregation.

These are vital questions that must be answered. How can God's children turn their hearts to Father Love in these last days, as Malachi 4:6 prophesies, if our words keep our Father from seeing us? How can our hearts return to our Father?

The Bible is full of examples of the cloak of invisibility. Joseph was made invisible when his jealous brothers threw him down into a well. This caused him to be hidden in a prison dungeon in Egypt. Officials could not see or hear his cause when a woman falsely accused him of sexual advances. God supernaturally removed the cloak because of His plan for Joseph, and he was made more than visible as the second in command in Egypt.

It is no surprise that the psalm of David that deals with rejection, Psalm 31, also involves invisibility, since the two often go hand in hand. David said that he had become a reproach, especially to his neighbors, and an object of dread to his acquaintances. He bemoaned, "Those who see me in the street flee from me. I am forgotten as a dead man, out of mind; I am like a broken vessel" (Ps. 31:11-12).

At times he even felt invisible to God: "As for me, I said in my alarm [panic], 'I am cut off from before Your eyes…'" (Ps. 31:22). He cried out, "My God, my God, why have you forsaken me? Far from my deliverance are the words of my groaning. O my God, I cry by day, but You do not answer; and by night, but I have no rest…" (Ps. 22:1-2).

In these verses David was speaking Satan's words. God hadn't really abandoned him. It just felt like it. We have all had times when we felt forsaken by God. And we have spoken similar words that became law and obliged Him to cooperate with the powerful words we spoke. We became at those times invisible to our Father.

Yet, praise God, our Father had foreseen the solution to this cloak of invisibility before time and the world began. He spoke of the *aleph-tav*, the Alpha and the Omega in the very first verse of the Bible. These powerful titles of Jesus were repeated in that verse, the second time with the letter that means nail in front of them. They prophesied that He would take the nails for us to pay the price of invisibility.

Jesus Took Our Cloak on Himself

But Jesus went beyond that. He spoke out the words David spoke, words that were this time a reality. He could no longer sense the presence of His Father who had been with Him from eternity. The man in Him felt the pain, and He cried out for the very first time in all His sufferings. This was the greatest hurt of all that He endured.

He couldn't even say, "Father." He cried, "My God, My God, why have You forsaken Me?" *Elohim* is a name for God, but it is not a personal name. Jesus took on the cloak of sin and the cloak of invisibility for us. He was separated from His Father so that we could call out, "Abba, Father."

Jesus came to reveal the Father. And He came to make us visible to our Father and His by His blood. He carried the grief and sorrows of invisibility for us (Isa. 53:4). He was "stricken, smitten of God, and afflicted" (same verse).

The Holy Spirit has revealed the process of our deliverance from this dreaded cloak. It took us a long time in many cases to open the door to this cloak. To see it removed, we need to understand what allowed it to be put on us in the first place. We need to lay down the pain of it on the new moon. We need to know how God wants us to break it off by the blood of Jesus.

Understanding this cloak will help us in many ways. We can avoid putting it on again, and we can help others start the process of its removal in their lives, their marriages, and their businesses.

Marriage counselors spend many hours helping people with relationship problems, but few counselors understand the root cause. Unforgiveness is a major issue. But what caused the unforgiveness in the first place? This cloak of invisibility is the cause of most divorces, but it has not been identified. God wants us to understand it. He wants to heal the marriages. And He wants to heal our hearts so they can turn to Him in this turbulent end time.

The Roots of Invisibility

In order to have a full understanding of this subject, we must realize that most individual cloaks of invisibility have their roots in childhood *rejection*. Parents speak words that make a child feel unloved and rejected. Other authority figures, grandparents, teachers, uncles, and aunts speak these words. They may be busy and so they say, "Get out of my sight." The child receives these words in his or her heart.

Between the ages of two and five children put a heavy demand on their parents, and parents will often speak words that make the child feel invisible. "Go away. Don't bother me. Go play somewhere else." These are examples of words of rejection, which is always present when the cloak is put on a child. The child feels, "Nobody wants me around."

Bonding is absent when the father does not cuddle the child when young. The child cannot smell the father's scent and be comforted by his presence. Hearing his voice causes the completion of the imprint of his voice when the child was in the womb. The birth was a traumatic experience, so the first reassurances they need are the voices of their parents. The mother was in stress and trauma during the delivery, so the child needs to hear the reassuring voice of the father especially. They need to be held by the father in the first three hours. If not, they expect to be rejected all their lives.

When the child approaches the tumultuous time of hormonal changes during the teen years, they need lots of hugs and words of acceptance. Often parents tell them they were unplanned, and these labels and curses enforce the cloak.

Negative *labels* cause a child to say, "Nobody wants, loves me, or recognizes me." He is sowing those words as part of his identity. Those words will enforce the "unlovability," "unwantedness," and the cloak of invisibility. Those labels, unless ripped off, will affect the child the rest of his life. The fear of being rejected and unloved will follow him.

Along with rejection and labels, *abuse* is another root of invisibility. When parents abuse children physically, verbally, sexually, spiritually, and in other ways, this is also a root of invisibility. They don't get the attention and affection for which they hunger. They will consequently do things to get that attention. They will continually test the parents to see if they really love them. They need the boundaries of discipline and love.

A parent may be drinking too much, taking out his frustration on the child. The child feels he in only a toy to be abused. The only way to avoid the abuse is to become invisible. The child seeks to be protected by the demon of invisibility, and the cloak will later form. It becomes protector and then a god to him.

"God doesn't want you anymore. If you disobey me, you are dishonoring your parent and you're going to suffer in hell." These are examples of spiritual abuse. Mental and spiritual abuse makes the child run to invisibility as his defender.

Children will leave toys on the floor to see their parents' reaction. It's not a deliberate defiance but a cry saying, "I need identity. I need to be seen. Does anybody know I'm here?" When a parent takes the toy away, the child has confirmed he is only a toy to be thrown away and rejected. If his toy is taken away, he feels he can also be thrown aside and is only a toy to be abused.

When a child fails a test in school, parents will sometimes ground the child for a week, causing him or her to feel like a failure and a criminal. This abuse brings on the cloak and causes negativity and doubt to enter their lives for good.

The "Fingernail on the Blackboard" Voice Nobody Likes

Mutaniak is a spirit that also enters into the invisibility equation. Your voice is heard as irritating, like the screech of a fingernail across a blackboard. People want to avoid hearing you. When your needs are not met, you start whining or crying. When you don't respond properly, you enforce the cloak and this screeching voice. The child will test the parents to see if their needs and desires will be met. When parents pray over their children before bed, they are blessed with a good night's sleep.

Our Father does not hear whiny prayers. We make ourselves invisible when we complain and whine to Him.

When children make gifts that parents don't properly receive with thanks, their feelings are hurt. They go to *mutaniak* as their defense. They begin to become tangential in their thinking rather than thinking conceptually. Yelling negativity into a child's life when he breaks a glass means you value that glass above your child. When they do a labor of love that is imperfect without any thanks, they declare themselves invisible. That desire for recognition turns children into tattletales.

Paul said when he did not have love, he became like "a noisy gong or a clanging cymbal" (1 Cor. 13:1). It works both ways. When a child doesn't receive love, he feels like a clanging cymbal, and will even sound like it with his whiny, attention-seeking tone.

We see so many throwaway children today because parents don't show them they love them. They smother them with the cloak of invisibility until they are totally rejected and abandoned. Our apostle, who received this revelation, knows this subject also from personal experience. For many years he ran a group home for abused and abandoned teens, and he has almost forty guardianship children along with his two biological children. He has counseled such situations for fifty years, apparently a Canadian record.

Bitterness is another part of this cloak of invisibility. The "everybody's done me wrong song" is the favorite tune of these people. They look for hidden motives or agendas that aren't really present. They are extremely suspicious. They can eventually be driven insane. Doctors give drugs to treat these psychoses, but it is a spiritual problem that can only be healed by the removal of the cloak in Jesus. That is the only way to heal the cause. They are only numbed because of the drugs that dull the brain.

Avoiding People at All Cost

Avoidance is another factor. People with this cloak go into hiding, "hermitism," and avoidance because of all the failure. They avoid areas where they feel controlled or rejected. They can't deal with these situations. Problems increase because of avoiding them. "I can't deal with that," they will say. "I don't want to discuss this." "I don't want to see _____ ever again." These phrases are from the spirit of avoidance, but they also strengthen the cloak.

"That doctor thought I was a joke. He doesn't understand or see my problem," some will say. They will consequently see problems that are not truly there, slipping sometimes into the spirit of hypochondria, feeling invisible when the doctor says, "I can't see anything wrong. It's in your mind." Avoidance is empowering these people to see these physical problems and to speak out "I can't, I won't, I don't, I'll never…" and other negative phrases.

The *"nobody knows the troubles I've seen"* syndrome of *loneliness* is another important factor in this cloak. The two main aspects of loneliness are the lack of ability to communicate your problems and no ability to be seen or understood. These people will ostracize themselves, creating a self-fulfilling prophecy.

They are seen as anti-social and thus have a hard time holding a job. They become a burden to the employer when they are employed. They develop the slave and victim mentality. A lonely person can't receive respect because they can't sow that respect into others' lives because they are invisible. They put the cloak over their mates.

"Unrecognizability" is another factor. They never trust people who give them a gift. They feel suspicious and fear that the person is after something from them or seeking control. They have a hard time responding to expression of thanks to them or congratulations. You have declared you will not be recognized, so you can't receive any recognition.

One competent bowler who rolled a perfect game could not receive the thousand-dollar check he earned. He thought he would have to repay by buying everybody a beer. They always see strings attached and ulterior motives to a gift.

They can't receive from their mates. They discourage their mates from giving to them. That mate doesn't therefore want to give and is made invisible. The offending mate thus receives a second, marital cloak of invisibility. Compassion is seen as a source of gossip. They seek sympathy, but if you show them sympathy, they see you as undermining them and treat you with contempt. They twist everything that is done to help them. They create arguments over nothing, creating pains of silence. Their marriages usually don't last long.

We need to pray for each other in this matter, since even when we lay down the cloak to Jesus, Satan will try to bring it back. That's why we need to understand what brings this cloak in.

"I Don't Want to Be Involved

Another aspect, common to all cloaks of invisibility, is a feeling of being left *uninvolved,* or "uninvolvable." This is a disturbing and confusing position for both parties, in any relationship, whether it is father-son, mother-daughter, or father-daughter. If a teenager develops this uninvolved approach in the cloak of invisibility, the parents say something and they are not heard, or they say, "Let's go do something," and the teen says, 'No, don't take me; I'm not interested,' and then they make everyone miserable along the way.

Family members, schoolteachers, and classmates have real difficulty dealing with those that have this uninvolved condition. They cannot become team members of anything. They can't work for a company and be part of an operation; they have to do things to corrupt the operation in one way or another. They feel that no matter what they do, it is unimportant, so they can do whatever they want.

This creates so many disturbing and confusing conditions for both parties involved, that they don't know how to handle one another. If you come down in a condemning way on them, they go tighter in their shell. If you try to encourage them out of their shell, they backbite you. They do want out, but they bite the hand that is pulling them out. The person with this cloak of invisibility attacks everybody that comes in contact with them with this "uninvolvement."

When you ask such people to do something, they say, "If you want that done, go do it yourself." Emptiness and incompleteness affect both parties because of the avoidance and the uninvolvement.

Our Cold and Disconnected World—and Church!

We as a society were meant to need each other. God made us to need one another, but we were meant to need Him most. So, if you become uninvolved in church functions, or uninvolved in going to Sabbath services, or going to Bible studies, what you are saying is that you don't want God involved in your life either. It is amazing how people who have this uninvolved attitude or spirit of mind are so good at avoiding doing what they know God wants them to do.

This uninvolvement brings in the spirit of murder. Murder attaches itself to both men and women, but more to men. They are uninvolved, but they see someone else who is involved receiving accolades. Jealousy sets in, and jealousy brings in the spirit of murder. We see this in the schools, where we see these students who were such quiet students, and all of a sudden, they start killing people. The spirit of murder shuts down the logic, judgmental, and moral sections. The more and more prevalent shooting sprees are the result.

When the demon leaves them, they can't believe that they did what they did. They think they were set up (and sometimes they are, as some see evidence of this in a recent movie theater shooting tragedy), and something happened; it just couldn't have been them. Along with the spirit of murder comes the spirit of hatred. It begins with hatred of self, and then hatred of everyone else. Then comes hatred of life, followed by hatred of God.

It's a progression. Hatred starts small, and the easiest one for a person to hate is him or herself. If he has been wrongly punished or accused for something, he avoids contact with those who have wronged him. He starts hating himself because he supposes nobody loves him. He then starts hating everyone else because he thinks, "I am always getting accused or I am being falsely charged."

Here's an example: "The person behind me was copying off my notes on a test and we both got zero because that person was copying my work and I didn't know about it." This injustice establishes the root of hatred, hatred for the other person that was cheating, but also hatred for the teacher and everyone else who got good marks. They begin to hate life and God. Being penalized for what you didn't do can leave you disenchanted with everything in life and bring in the blanket of hopelessness.

Coldness sets in. Some refer to this as the dead fish syndrome. When you are uninvolved, you cannot receive love. A person goes to give you a hug, and the back and neck stiffens and you "unhug" the person. People tend to avoid coldness, even in a physical sense. Ever seen anyone sunbathing at minus forty degrees in a Canadian winter?

The colder a person becomes under this uninvolvement, the more everyone around them avoids them. It creates a "cold fish syndrome," and even if they get married later on, they never try to please anyone else, including their mates.

Common Curses Uncommonly Broken

The last factor in creating the cloak is called the *common curse.* Examples are:

- I never want to see you again.
- I hate the sight of you.
- I wish you were never born.
- We just can't see each other ever again.
- If I live to be a thousand, I never want to see you again.
- You are so whiny that it is easier to sleep next to a generator working on overload than it is to be next to you.
- With your luck, you will get lost and never find your way to my door again.
- Get lost.
- Do the world a favor and jump off a bridge.
- Children are to be seen and not heard. (This means that any opinion, want, need, or any love you want to express is blocked. You must stand or sit quietly and not say or do anything until you are told to do so. You are told what to think, what to say, and what to do.)
- Why not take a long walk off a short pier?
- Do I have to have _____ on my team? Can't he be on someone else's team? For my last choice, I guess I have to choose you, since there is nobody else left.

- If I had a choice of living with a bear, a thousand rattlesnakes, or you, I would always pick the bear and the rattlesnakes.
- I wouldn't marry you if you were the last person on earth!

These are simple curses, but they give legal right for the cloak of invisibility. They all have to be broken off, and if you said them, you must rescind them in Jesus' name and pray blessings upon the person you cursed so as to avoid backlash from the curse.

These curses have the effect of making a person put on the cloak of invisibility. They destroy hope and destroy a person's character. They also destroy a person's will to live as an overcomer or as a builder, one who can succeed and bring forth increase. All curses put you under the power of betrayal, unforgiveness, infirmity, and invisibility.

Change Your Hiding Place to Jesus!

This cloak of invisibility is not only destroying our society, but it is destroying the church. It is stopping people from seeing themselves as part of God's family, as children of God. Jesus prophesied this coldness of heart in the last days, saying, "most people's love will grow cold" (Mat. 24:12), and the context shows He is talking about church people.

What would be the limits of the church if we all laid down to Jesus all aspects of invisibility? The church would shine like the light she is prophesied to be in Isaiah 60. That light would bring a great, end-time harvest of souls that would be inspired by seeing believers in Jesus set free.

It's time we laid down invisibility to Jesus on the new moon. While we may have received the cloak when we were quite young and without much defense, we have kept accepting it all our lives. We must recognize where we have sought refuge under a demonic cloak rather than seeking to hide in Jesus.

David told Jesus, "You are my hiding place…" (Ps. 32:7). He is waiting for us to hide under the shadow of His wings so we can "sing for joy" (Ps. 63:7). And we should do just that, praise with joyous song when we do the break off communion of this cloak of invisibility.

Lay Down Item Checklist

We were recently reminded of an important aspect of the cloak of invisibility to lay down to Jesus on the new moon: we should turn over the loss of contact with the Holy Spirit and our inability to be seen by God and to walk hand-in-hand with Jesus.

A clock of invisibility from a pastor puts the demon unworthiness in charge of the cloak. And when the congregation sends it, the demon "unwantedness" is in charge of it and determines the way it functions. This situation often occurs in churches with cliques where people are excluded from the popular cliques. These cloaks are often fixed securely by spells. Other aspects of invisibility include:

- Rejection present
- Inability to bond
- Unlovable labels
- Being invisible to God, loss of contact with the Holy Spirit and being able to walk hand-in-hand with Jesus
- The devaluation caused by the cloak
- Abuse
- Mutaniak—the demon that causes a whiny tone in your voice that sounds like screeching fingernail sounds over a blackboard
- Bitterness—turns others off; creates psychiatric disorders
- Avoidance—we agree with those who want to avoid us; leads to hiding, living in your fantasies; grows like cancer; "I cannot deal with that…" puts you into failure mode
- Loneliness and victim mentality
- Unrecognizability—avoid receiving gifts, congratulations; with compliments — "What are they after?" brings in contempt, seeing just the negative side of things; always in discouraged and discouraging mode

- "Left uninvolved or uninvolvable" (common to all invisibility); brings in spirit of murder (especially men) --common in mass murders; hatred of self and others, of life and of God as this hatred progresses
- Erosion— loss of confidence because you can't hear encouraging words
- Self-involvement because of being uninvolved with others; some in India actually contemplate their navels; perverted pleasure comes with self-involvement; quite hard to bring these people back to reality
- Brooding—must figure out everything that could go wrong before you act; brings...
- Regrets – "couda, wouda, shouda" ...putting dreads on a pedestal
- Dreads- dread being seen, which brings back all of the above...
- Contempt
- Vendetta comes along without fail
- Voyeurism
- Dreamscaping
- Willingness to lie
- Infidelity - unable to carry out commitments expeditiously or correctly; can't focus on the request; activates multiple personalities
- "The Common Curse" - "I never want to see you again." "I hate the sight of you." "We can't see each other ever again," all of which enforce the cloak of invisibility. "Get lost." "Do the world a favor, and jump off a bridge." "Children are to be seen and not heard." (Any opinion, want, need, or love to give or receive cannot be expressed.) "Do I have to have Joe on my team?" "I guess we'll take you; you're last." "I wouldn't marry you if you were the last person on earth." These common curses destroy hope of overcoming and destroy character. They put you under the power of invisibility and betrayal (with unforgiveness and infirmity).

Below is the format for breaking off the cloak of invisibility over individuals. We recommend the agreement of four believers in total to take communion together as you agree on these words once you have blessed the unleavenened bread and wine or juice to be the body and blood of Jesus. Certain grocery stores sell unleavened bread or crackers with no yeast added.

Communion Service for Release from Individual Cloak

Father, our Eternal Loving God, we rejoice that You are God and that You have called us to Jesus and to our freedom. For today we seek freedom from the cloak (comforter) of invisibility, and freedom from its anchors, tie downs, wrong understanding, wrong perceptions, wrong attitudes, wrong evaluations, and the burdens of a false identity that living with invisibility has caused.

We acknowledge that we established the roots for the cloak (comforter) by accepting and defining ourselves by rejection and its lies; by labels and their lies; by the obtrusiveness of others (we have let others in their anger say something that got into our heart so it created lies of identity); by the sounds of mutuniak (screeching, strident sound) and his lies; by bitterness and his lies; by the fears of avoidance and all his lies; by the fears of loneliness and all his lies; by the spirit of unrecognizability (that we don't perceive something so we don't recognize it); by the spirit of uninvolvement and all his lies and most of all by the common curses with which I define myself and all the lies I spoke to create them.

With these in place we let betrayal, unforgiveness, and infirmity nail these roots to our souls and therefore, make Your words, Father, seem meaningless to us.

We reject all claims of these roots and confess our sins of unbelief that had established them.

We ask Your forgiveness, Father, and we forgive ourselves for establishing and maintaining these roots as well as for the effect of these roots by refusing Your gifts and missing the mark, purpose, and vision you have for us.

We thank You, Father, for this forgiveness of our loss of contact with You, because of these roots.

We reject and release all aspects of common cursing that have brought the cloak (comforter) upon us.

We rescind all words spoken that established it upon those around us, including all words of hate, dismissal, abortion and contempt.

We reject accepting the words, "I never want to see you again," and release our agreement with them, whether we spoke them or they were spoken over us.

We rescind and release those over whom we have spoken such words.

We call forth Your spirit of forgiveness to touch everyone involved.

We reject the accepting of the "get lost," or "never come to my door again" type of statements. We release their hold on our life and those around us, and we forgive those who spoke the words.

We release and reject the cause and curses of children to be silent and invisible.

We rescind our words of agreement and our complacency in being uninvolved.

We reject and release all words that made us feel worthless, useless, and hopelessly incompetent. We forgive all issuers of such words.

We release and reject all chains of denial that have bound us to false notions and left us open to insidious attacks.

We thank You, Father, that our eyes are open to understanding cause and effect.

We acknowledge our reliance on things for a false sense of security, such as people, places, things, ideas, or doctrines that kept us bound in these webs of lies. We hid from You, Father, Jesus, Holy Spirit, and the correction of Your Word of truth.

We forgive ourselves as well as those who opened the door by their words for us to live in hiding even from ourselves.

We acknowledge the pain that brought in loss, madness, anger/rage, irrationalism, vindictiveness, irresponsibility and the pulling up good roots, in breaking vows and denying responsibility. We also confess the pain that caused the disregard for others; the need for control; sympathy seeking; avoidance of reality checks; the releasing of accusation and the assuming guilt on others. This drove isolationism to new heights. We turn over the pain and ask for Your forgiveness Father and the forgiveness of those we have injured.

We acknowledge the doors we opened to self-deception that brought us to the making of debt, shame, fears, and fact inversion into God-like status.

We assumed sin, motivation, and intents against us as real attacks (When you misread somebody or their intent, you can make the most innocent thing seem guilty. We victimize in order to confirm our self-deceptions. We keep victimizing these people until they do what we assumed they were going to do.)

Father, we seek forgiveness for this self-delusional fantasy of wrongs that caused others to stumble, to run from Jesus, and to curse.

We acknowledge the confusion and pain we caused others by expecting them to be mind readers—expecting them to know the unspoken fears that cause stress for everyone around us. (Do not expect others to read your mind, but tell them what is on your mind. Then accept correction. These things steal peace from us, from our home, and our family life.)

We release, reject, and rescind all words that demanded others to be mind readers of our expectations and demands. We ask Your forgiveness on this matter.

We acknowledge our need to blame everyone but ourselves for the choices we make as we claim all setbacks are someone else's fault. We have kept ourselves outside the circle of love and opened the door to loss, failure, accident, anger/rage, hatred and even the desire to murder. We ask Your forgiveness, Father, for this oppressive approach and the hurt it has caused others.

We acknowledge living by the rules of "why me?" We've been self-consumed, self-involved, and self-proclaimed, declaring everything that doesn't go our way as unfair, a set up, or a conspiracy. (In this we really have to examine ourselves. The "why me?" syndrome is easy for us to bypass because it requires us to look at where we have said, "This is unfair.")

As soon as we declare something as unfair we are immediately in the "why me?" syndrome. We have to acknowledge that this is one of the things that brings in and maintains the cloak of invisibility. When we move into the unfair syndrome, if we don't turn it over to Jesus on the cross, we will always call the cloak of invisibility back.) We ask You, Father, for Your forgiveness, and we forgive ourselves for not recognizing this. We ask for the discernment in this matter.

We acknowledge our earthly father's rejection when we could not meet his unspoken expectations or qualifications in the most perfect manner. We know the pain of emptiness that it brought in and the longing for encouragement and acceptance. We therefore disconnected Your love, Father, because of it. Our soul was distressed with failure, infirmity, overwhelming it constantly so we have had great trouble trusting You. We seek Your forgiveness for this. With our father's rejection in place we allowed invalidation to annul the opportunities that we found in our life. (People are given ideas all the time of how to be rich, or how to stay out of trouble. The Holy Spirit speaks to you all the time. Invalidation causes you to hear the Holy Spirit less and less. You don't allow your heart to receive what He is speaking.)

Everything You said, Father God, was responded to with "I can't." That became a controlling factor in dealing with all challenges in life and in negating our self-worth. For this we ask Your forgiveness.

We ask Your forgiveness for declaring ourselves burdens or burden bearers. We acknowledge that Jesus is the Bearer of our burdens and that we need to lay down our burdens, cares, and concerns to Him. We have failed in this, letting ourselves be burdened as though we were our own savior, our own deliverer, and the deliverer of others. We blocked our blessings by doing this. We have thus also blocked the blessings to come on others, since we weren't encouraging others to turn things over to Jesus.

Father, we acknowledge the implanting of the rug, or what is called the rug syndrome, and it's pull to do evil or to hide from the truth, to be buried in debt, to be enclosed in addictions, to be set in place for walking over, to be buried by the sins and to be choked on the dust of doubt. (The dust we collect is that choking dust of doubt.) We see denial as laying this rug over the cloak of invisibility. We seek Your forgiveness for establishing this rug in order to stay away from Your knowledge.

We acknowledge that we have made the wet blanket available to abuse us into accepting the loss of morality, integrity, and steadfastness. We condemned, labeled, and accused those who sought to walk Your way in Jesus. We seek Your forgiveness for this and for the mental problems it has caused.

We acknowledge that invisibility has changed our identity to the "screaming I." We have lost who we were supposed to become and we have become self- centered, self- absorbed, and seeking to build self-esteem. We recognize that this has blocked or stolen our healing, our wealth, our families, our peace, and our contentment. We got into a state of frustration and intolerance, self-focusing so that distrust abounded to others and to You. We put the cloak of invisibility on others, without mercy or compassion.

Under the cloak of invisibility we acknowledge we have developed a wicked heart that refuses to receive the words of peace, always fault finding, seeking control, defiant to Your anointed, full of accusation, judgmentalism, and lustful, wishful wants. Our bodies even fight against us because the wicked heart is too much for it to bear. (This is one of the causes of heart attacks, strokes, and total shut down of the body.)

The Bible says the heart is deceitful above all things, and who can know it? When you are under the cloak you can't know your own heart. You need Jesus. A wicked heart causes extreme stress and extreme tension and deforms people. Even young people are bent over, the weight of sin being too much to bear.

Father, with You all things are possible. We need You to change us and heal our hearts. We need Jesus to take off all the layers of the cloaks of invisibility with its roots, agents, ties, deception, pains, and false identities. We turn this over to Jesus as well. We need Jesus to clean the wicked heart and to destroy the wet blanket and the smothering rug.

Father, renew a right spirit in us. Give us the knowledge, wisdom, understanding, discernment, and peace to reject these blankets so we never call them back. We need the healing stripes of Jesus to heal us in body, brain, and soul so we can walk in Your love.

We thank You Father for our freedom from this cloak (comforter) of invisibility and for Your love in giving us Jesus. All power, glory and honor be Yours forever. In Jesus' name, amen.

CHAPTER 18

Avoid the Pain of Divorce! — Read This Now

The Real Cause of Divorce: Marital Invisibility

The cloak of invisibility is affecting unawares more and more people, especially in marriage. All the causes of divorce can be summed up in this marital cloak of invisibility. Many terms are used in describing the causes of marriage problems: incompatibility, financial disputes, and intimacy anorexia. Mates are said to be too busy for their partner. Nevertheless, all of these problems stem from the root cause: one mate is making the other invisible and putting that cloak over them. It's a spiritual entity that must be broken off with the proper procedure. You have come to the place where it is understood and you can learn to deal with it.

Often there is already an existing invisibility present over both partners in the marriage, and they come into the relationship out of sympathy for the other in invisibility. They then put up a wall that literally prevents them from seeing the other person. It's a nasty situation.

Let's look at some of the conditions that establish the cloak, or what it does to you, as we relate an actual excerpt of one of our radio programs on freedomtruthseekers.com as Charley West interviews our apostle, identified in A, meaning answer:

1) You become a *fixture outside the circle of love.* A picture diagram would be a dot in the middle of a circle, being the mate, and a dot outside that

circle being you, compared to where they are. You are not in their circle of influence or their circle of love. So if you are a permanent fixture outside their circle, you have the cloak of invisibility. What it means is that you are gradually cut out of the other person's love life, their regular life and activities such as their job or sports. You are disconnected from the marriage and from all involvement of the financial affairs of that relationship.

Question from radio host Charley West: So the person who is excluded in all the ways you just mentioned, they could be thinking that the other person is creating these things and putting up the wall rather than realizing that is them who have the cloak of invisibility over them, which is affecting the mate?

A: Yes, and usually what happens is that if one person enters the marriage with the cloak of invisibility, the other person will take on a cloak of invisibility after a very short period of time. The root behind that is that the two become one flesh. As soon as they have an argument in which they curse one another, Satan is allowed to get in, and the curses that are over one, now come over the other. This becomes a touchy situation because they don't want to see themselves as being the root of what the other person is doing to them or what they are doing to the other person.

Charley: Us being in our fleshy humanist state, in our pride, want to see it from another point of view instead.

A: Yes, and that is why you become a fixture outside that circle of love, because of not wanting to acknowledge it (and not wanting the other person's involvement in helping you out of it).

An example of this is Prince Charles' situation. Time has gone by, and his mom has stayed on as queen for so long already, and he figures that her health is so good that she could probably reign another twenty to thirty years before he would get a chance to reign, and he would be pretty old by then. So what happened was as he was growing up, parents tended to make children be seen and not heard. They were taught to put on a good face, play this little role, and do this thing or that thing. And this is a common thing found in those of German, Ukrainian or Russian background. What people don't realize is that Queen Victoria is of German background, and the Windsor family has carried this cloak of invisibility and put it over their children, generation after generation after generation. The Queen is unable to break that cloak off her children; she would have to take it off of herself first. The effect was that it would cause a rupture in her marriage and her children's marriages, like a divorce because of this invisibility.

This person becomes unseen as a person or part of anything good. They can be part of something bad happening, but they are not seen as part of something good. You literally get blamed for things, because you are so much "divorced" from the other person's life that they see you as the hindrance to their development, not as a support to their development. Even if you are supporting them whole-heartedly they cannot receive it that way.

Usually what happens is that one of the persons will have a narcissistic personality (a strong self-centered focus). Usually what happens is that the person with the cloak of invisibility will be drawn to someone who has this narcissistic syndrome in his or her personality. It may not be fully developed but it is there. So when we have this unseen person, you could walk in front of them naked and they wouldn't notice. You may as well not be there. This cloak of invisibility is a detriment to anyone in a relationship, and a bad one. And it is getting more and more common because of many stresses we have going on in our society.

2) You are *not heard*. You are like a static noise as is created by the spirit *mutaniak.*

Mutaniak is a word from ancient writings of psychology that understood and named this condition. It recognizes that sometimes or with some people, they have spoken but are literally not heard, even though the other person was listening. It is a condition caused by an interference of a demon we call the *mutaniak* spirit. It disrupts the pathway or process of audibility. Vocally words are spoken clearly but when this spirit is attacking one or both of the people, the hearing of the words can sound like static noise. It can be an irritating, scratchy sound like scratching on a black board for an exaggeration of the higher pitch of a woman's voice, or it can be a demeaning, lording-over, oppressive kind of voice that is an exaggeration of a man's deeper voice. So the words themselves that are said can be completely appropriate, but when this disruption to the listener takes charge, then the proper message is not relayed. So it is true as taught again and again, that it is not what is said but "how" it is said that people have a problem with. The "how" in this case is unintentional. The speaker hears himself as giving a proper message, but the listener hears a distorted version. Another way that this gets twisted even more is when a person is speaking with a tone of voice from being attacked in other ways that has shifted their personality accepting that they are somehow a victim needing to defend themselves. This together with *mutaniak* will always result in great confusion of the messages. Another known trait of *mutaniak* is that it goes on as a generational curse, unless it is recognized and prayed out of existence for the victim and his family line.

Mutaniak refers to an irritating noise as in a scratching on a black board. The one listening is already agitated by not being at peace within their soul and so when a person with the spiritual cloak of invisibility speaks to their mate or children, they are tuned out. This is what makes it so difficult to get information across, because those who are supposed to listen are turned right off. It is a natural format occurrence of having this cloak of invisibility.

Charley: So at that stage a person with the cloak on is not necessarily just tuned out by their mate or children but it would actually affect everybody in their life.

A: It would eventually effect everyone around them, extended family, acquaintances, etc. because this spirit of *mutaniak* makes it impossible to hear them. It is like listening to a radio station with screeches on it; they will tune it out or turn it off.

3) *Not respected or appreciated as an individual*; maybe as a slave laborer, or a bed-slave, or as a babysitter but they are not respected as an individual or that they have individual needs. Their need to be nourished in their relationship in the marriage is not available. The cloak blocks it out *or*

the other person is blocked from providing it. The mate is blocked from the thoughts of giving this.

4) *They are not allowed to be involved in the normal affairs of the family.* Whether it is the projects to do around the house and yard, or the financial dealings, their opinion is not included or it is considered they are not allowed to have one. It is like they are told what there will be and they need to be satisfied (a "do this and you will like this" approach). That is very strong over some of these cultural backgrounds who have been putting this cloak of invisibility over their children for generations.

5) *They are not considered, whether it is a new idea or way of doing things.* They are excluded if their way is different from the ways of the other person. With this cloak they are not a part of their mate's life. So they are still operating as two separate individuals when they should come together as one. They are not considered valid. Their ideas, contributions or needs are not valid. This rejection thickens the covering of this cloak over them and their life.

6) *They aren't cherished.* Anything that they do, is considered a minimal effort or not worth recognizing. No matter how much they try to please their mate, it is never seen as good enough.

For example: a husband and wife were planning to buy a house. The wife (having the cloak of invisibility) had a part-time job besides raising the children to help raise money for their purchase. Remember that whatever the person does under the cloak of invisibility, it never ends up good enough, so if the down payment was $15,000, and they came up with $14,795, then it is thought that they didn't do their part. Then it is considered that they should not be part owner of that property or that development of that family. If they don't provide 100% contribution, then they don't get considered at all. This has been responsible for many divorces.

As long as they are not part of doing something for the family or for the marriage, then the title of marriage becomes, "this is my wife" (or husband), but not "this is my partner," not their best friend, not the person I like to be with, not even the person I like; it is the person I have to endure. This aspect of not cherishing is very important.

I know of a situation where the husband and wife (who had this cloak over her) had a business. It was just paying for itself. The wife came in and got things organized and updated with the billings and collections, and it became more profitable. As soon as it became profitable then she wasn't wanted around anymore, and it was concluded that she didn't know anything about business. Even though she was the key person to benefit the situation, the spirit of invisibility caused a diminishment. The spouse, in selfishness, will consider it to be "my" success and "you are the anchor that I drag around with me."

7) *They are not acknowledged for their emotions, pain, work or contributions.* For example a mother spends a lot of her time taking care of the children, preparing meals, house cleaning and laundry, and making sure that the bills are being paid, and the husband comes in seeing things orderly and says "look, you don't do anything around the house anyway." So all the effort put in so that there was a good functioning home for him to come home to was not appreciated or acknowledged. This is very diminishing for a person and it causes a pain that the other person does not acknowledge because with this invisibility over them is heard as more noise or static to their mate. It becomes a broken down relationship. The fact that they have emotions is a drawback to them; it may occupy some of their time. The emotions of the person under this cloak become unseen or not valid. Even counselors and physiatrists can miss this person's pain because of this invisibility.

8) *Not welcomed.* They become a sore at family gatherings, or used as a decoration at reunions, celebrations or business events. They add to the function because they look like they have a normal belonging, especially for their mate and their family to count them in, as in doing their duty to include them. They are a number. They are not a useful, contributing factor otherwise.

9) *They are not encouraged or thanked.* They are not helped to grow in any area of their life. No compliments, adoration, or appreciation for all the extras that they do for the family.

10) *Not part of one's circle of activity.* Not only left out but not invited in. For example, you're going to the gym after work and not saying that you were. Supper is ready and you can't be reached at the office, not here and not there. What's it to you? You are nobody. That is a sign that you are left out. Not an active member of anything.

11) *Not fed as a partner or a family member.* You're treated as a kicking dog for others frustration, or a workhorse or a field animal. You're not a part of the activities of that partner, therefore not treated as a partner in anything. Money can be handed over and told go buy something to keep them quiet, without proper time and attention shared with them.

This is the cause of so many divorces, this cloak of invisibility. Whether in the church or not, the root of most divorces comes where one partner is operating out of pure selfishness, and the other one is used or abused. The problem is that most churches don't recognize this whole aspect of this cloak of invisibility. There is enough about it in the Bible, but most often they deal with the common differences between men and women instead.

12) *Taken for granted like a mist or fog in the morning,* or like the trash that builds up and you haven't taken it out yet, or a bad odor that is there temporarily. A selfish or narcissistic personality doesn't realize that they are a part of the cause of that bad odor. When a person is taken for granted, they realize that nothing they do is ever good enough to be acknowledged and what they do is expected not appreciated (like a computer program, it is always doing its job repetitiously without anyone noticing its important role).

13) *The invisible one is always being taken advantage of without gratitude. praise or pay.* This is a common occurrence with housewives and stay-at-home moms. They are expected to fulfill the whole role full of

responsibilities, and what do they receive in return for doing this? Normally when you sow, you also reap. What happens under invisibility is that the good that was reaped because of what you sowed, your mate says, "Look what I have done."

14) *Given unspoken expectations or expected to read your mate's mind* because communication is always lacking or minimal. When you don't do as the other expected, they come back with negative reactions, mutterings, barbs, innuendos or insinuations.

Whole nations and races of people exist with this cloak of invisibility on them where proper communication is not happening, and is impossible because of this cloak. Our First Nations people here in Canada had this cloak put on them by Noah, when he cursed Canaan, because they are all sons of Canaan (a son of Ham and grandson to Noah). There is much fighting among themselves or fighting for recognition without satisfaction. They don't realize why or what the root of it is.

15) *Given blame and no credit for the good that happens when you've put work into it.* This is a little different than not being encouraged. What I'm talking about is assumed failure, like " I figured you would foul that up anyway", or "I knew I couldn't trust you to do this right", or "If you had done this thing or that, then this wouldn't have happened". The spouse replies, "But you didn't tell me that you wanted this done, or in that specific way".

This last point is something that adds significantly to the power of this cloak of invisibility. It's like being wrapped up in it and they even lose their own identity, or they can't believe they are even loved by God. The main purpose of this spiritual cloak of invisibility is to teach them to believe that they are unlovable.

16) *Given rejection, and expected to live in happiness as though it were normal.* They are expected to live in loneliness, lameness from being avoided because they have such limited identity, and limited value as a person. They are continually reminded that they are rejects and that

nothing they do is good enough, and their ideas are not good enough. It's important to remember is that they are under constant rejection.

17) *Given labors, burdens, or assignments without recognition of that person's needs.* Taking care of children is a labor. Taking care of a spouse that doesn't take care for you is a labor.

Your mate says things to you that burden you down with no release and no forgiveness, so it continues to get piled on. It would eventually come to a point, if there isn't a divorce, that the mate will have a mental breakdown where there is a disconnecting of the mind and the brain in many areas. They become almost incapable of carrying things out, or they may go into a state of hysteria. This is where the burdens become so draining that there is no peace left in their life. It's as if they are screaming in pain, but it is taken in a form of *mutaniak*, like static noise and not heard. A vicious cycle is taking place.

18) *They are given a cover like a crawl.* A husband is supposed to be a covering for his wife, to protect her and cherish her, but if he is cherishing his parents or his job or business or his extra-curricular activities, then this crawl or cloak begins to close in so that there is no way for them to see an escape route or how to move forward. This diminishes their hope, and hopelessness sets in to such a degree that they can become unable to deal with normal things of life. Usually the familiar or routine things can be continued but even to accomplish them requires much more thought and energy so everything takes longer. Then the spouse and others can conclude that this person is unable to do more, or lazy, or that they are even defying their role.

Charley: Would that allow addictions to take over as well?

A: Definitely, addictions could take place, or they can turn to whining, crying, complaining, and be in deep bitterness. Holding all of these emotions within ends up strengthening the cloak's grip onto like welding points to the spirit of unforgiveness with its tormentors. Eventually unforgiveness locks them in so tightly that they see no escape. That vicious cycle we mentioned previously turns all conversations and actions with their spouse into a frenzy of confusion and disharmony. This is where in psychology or counseling circles they call the insensitive spouse the "crazy-maker". Everything does seem crazy to those under this kind of invisibility, and it can look like they are the ones developing a mental instability. A Christian book explaining this is called "The Crazy-Makers".

19) *There is no "we", "us" or "our" in any of the things of the marriage.* The spouse will refer to all things as "I", "me" and "my"; "this is what I have done", "I have done this by myself", "I've raised these children all by myself". Typically a wife can be considered like a babysitter, a cook, or be the housekeeper, but the two cannot become one. When this occurs it is usually when the mate enforcing the invisibility has not been able to cut the apron strings with the parents, so is not able to let the spouse become part of them. The person that is enforcing the cloak feels like they are doing their duty by supplying that person a place to stay, not that they have taken them on to be a part of who they are.

When the man has this cloak of invisibility, he sees himself as being a tool, a repairer, or the money supplier, or a receptacle for hostility and cursing— not part of a new union of marriage. When there is no "we", "us" and "our" there can be no balance of acceptance of their mate by their family line. If they themselves don't accept their spouse as a valid person, it is doubtful that their parents or the siblings will accept them, and many other members of the family will also fail to see that spouse as a valid member of that family. So they are married as an outsider.

Often what happens is the head of that family line refuses to bless the incoming daughter or son to be a part of his family. It should be that he would lay hands upon them and give his blessing of taking on the family name, that he receives them equally as one of his own children into his family circle of love and belonging. This should be done on both sides of the family and then there is an equal or balanced acceptance because both are welcomed into both family lines.

If that wasn't done, it increases the power of this cloak of invisibility. It is more difficult if one or more of those parents are dead. Avoidance or failure to do so is detrimental to the relationship and very likely could lead to divorce, or cause a situation where a couple continues to live together but they tolerate one another and don't love one another. This blessing is an open door for love to flow because love was passed onto them, sowing the seed of love into the new relationship.

The unblessed partner becomes the focal point of most problems that arise then in that family. Usually all blame, hostility, and condemnation goes to the one who has had the cloak of invisibility reinforced upon them by not being accepted.

Then that couple usually resort to living a lie, or role-playing, or pretending, mind-games, etc. for attention because there is no true affection. So eventually neither end up in each other's circle of love and the children can eventually end up outside of either or both circles of love, as well as even becoming outside of grandparent's circle and other extended family's circle as well.

Invisibility leaves you emotionally stranded or demeaned for having feelings or meaningful, valid thoughts or premonitions.

With this cloak, you don't get validated as a person. No one will hear you or accept your word, your warnings, your independent thoughts or you seeing things in a different light. And yet that is what marriage is all about: two people with different points of view being able to come together to work things out, and where both learn to get rid of selfishness in order to eliminate the narcissistic approach to life.

A comment that is often made is that one mate is not responsible for the other's happiness, and that is true; it would be like role-playing if you did. However, you can be responsible for your mate's sadness, losses, or feelings of rejection, and their cloak of invisibility. You could even be responsible for them living in unforgiveness.

20) *Not encouraged to expand one's talents or horizons.* A characteristic of the cloak of invisibility from your mate is to keep you boxed in. When you try to step out of that box, you are ostracized or somehow have people's criticism and disapproval coming down on you, like one who is tied up at a stake to be burnt. So when you are undermined for everything you are doing, unforgiveness sets in and one becomes bound

to the tormentors. Pain is built up from all the different people treating you this way, and it overflows and overflows, as all of these points all get welded onto this person. They begin to feel trapped with no escape, like falling into a well and having no footholds to push yourself back up.

21) *Exaggerations and false conclusions.* The person under this cloak tries to get a point across, and the other person hates that point and exaggerates it into a false conclusion, or reacts in an exaggerated opposition. Anything new or different that the narcissistic person has not thought of is deemed as a threat and therefore a very unfavorable response is given. It's the typical black or white with no in between, or one far side of the ditch or the other. Now, the one trying to get the information across feels like they are beached, washed up on dry land, sun baked, and then picked apart by seagulls. This continual occurrence is a setup for anger and despair.

22) Under all of the above attacks, and everything being exaggerated, the next one is a *twisting of the information* and the person with invisibility is said to be the cause of this, too. Their own information is twisted and used against them or for the other person's benefit.

Can you see Satan's fingerprints all over this when you learn what this cloak is and what it does? It has been destroying marriages and any other relationships as well. It is just a matter of time before it does. Some people have more endurance capacity or prayers are being said for them, but it still forces them into unforgiveness. When you are in this situation, it can grow like a cancer. And indeed a major root of cancer is unforgiveness. It is a cancer, a destroying and killing cancer.

Marital Invisibility Communion

Now we proceed to the happy solution, the breaking off of this deadly problem of the cloak of invisibility in communion. Eight believers are suggested for this important breakoff.

This is the part where the details from the initial statements about marital invisibility are now spoken in a prayer to the Father to receive and allow these things to be turned over to Jesus. When we hold onto any part of it, we actually block the removal of the cloak of invisibility. It will come back eventually in full force again stronger. So unless you are willing to deal with this as a whole unit, the release from it doesn't happen.

When we deal with this cloak of invisibility, we have to realize that it affects every area of our life. And now, the following is a guide or sample prayer to allow the turnover of the pain and losses and suffering one would likely have experienced. It is quite a long one and you may have to go over it two or three times. It is something you really have to release from your heart. You must be specific and firm as you speak, taking these pains from your heart and turn them over to Jesus at the cross. The ideal time for this is the new moon.

Now the prayer:

Father, forgive me, for I have enabled my spouse, (say his/her name in the blanks), to place upon me the cloak of invisibility. I haven't walked in Your given identity, Your forgiveness, and Your love because of it. And I ask now for Your grace of forgiveness in releasing these pains, and Your grace in releasing my past, and all the effects of invisibility to Jesus on the cross.

Father, I choose to turn over to Jesus the false identity that I have accepted, or that I played, that was expected of me. I reject this false identity as being a fixture outside of (____) circle of love, our normal family life and of marriage intimacy and involvement. I forgive (____) for making me a fixture outside of his/her circle of love and life, and I forgive (____) for all the pain that he/she caused that is now upon Jesus and the cross, because He has taken it from me.

This cloak of invisibility has made me see myself and be seen by others as a tool, not as a loved spouse or parent but something to be used, abused, and wasted. I choose to forgive my spouse for labeling me and cloaking me, and I turn over the pain and all its affects to Jesus.

Father, this cloak of invisibility has caused me not to be heard by my mate, my children, or my friends. I even think that the spirit of *mutaniak* has made me sound like static noise or a scraping on a chalkboard in his/her ears. I choose to forgive (___) and all who couldn't hear the real me or acknowledge my pain. I hereby turn over this pain to Jesus upon the cross. I forgive them, and I turn it over.

Invisibility made me feel disrespected, unacceptable, and unappreciated. As a person and as an individual, I felt like an after-thought, an attachment or an appendage, with no purpose but to be dangled as a toy for amusement for others. I have chosen to turn over this pain and to forgive (_____) and all who used me or saw me in this way.

Father, I have felt excluded from involvement in family matters and from events in (_____)'s life. I have seen myself as one that everyone avoids as soon as important matters came up. Invisibility caused me to be shunned, and also my abilities, causing great pain and no self-worth. I didn't feel like I was valuable to anybody with this cloak of invisibility. Life took on a lifelessness, a hopelessness, and pain upon pain over time, and it has increased. I have had regrets every day that I have lived with my mate. I now choose to forgive my mate, and turn over all the pain of exclusion. I turn this over to Jesus for He is my Redeemer and my Savior in all things.

Invisibility drove stakes through my hands and my soul so that I was not allowed to get involved, not considered a legitimate member of my family or (_____)'s family or in my own home, or in our business, or my church. Nothing in (_____)'s life felt open to me, and it spread out to others around me that doors were also closing with them as well. I choose to forgive (_____) and all those that didn't see me and didn't allow me to be involved, and contribute and to share. I turn this pain over to Jesus and seek His fullness.

When others were hugged or kissed, I never received anything that made me feel cherished. I was never made to feel part of (_____)'s life or in the things that really counted. Ambitions, hopes, and dreams of (_____) were all kept secret.

Invisibility made me seem like the cow for slaughter, never where I felt that I could be the one to be celebrated but that I was the one cut apart at another person's feet. I choose to forgive (_____) and all of them who thought I was not worthy to be cherished. I turn this pain over to Jesus, and I claim it no more.

Father, my pain, emotions, feelings and even contributions were not acknowledged by (_____) or when I was given the silent treatment, and still expected to understand things. I had hatred towards everyone who ignored me, everything that I had to do with them, and I even had hatred towards You, Father. The distress of this invisibility led me into trying to fix things my own way, by my own strength, my own power, and my own wisdom. I had done and said things I never wanted to say or do. The more I did things my way, the more frustrated and distressed I became, until the cloak of invisibility made me invisible even to myself. Father, I choose to forgive (_____) and everyone who treated me with no acknowledgement and enabled the pains of distress to conquer me. I turn these pains over to Jesus on the cross, for I cannot bear them any longer, and I know Jesus has already paid for them.

When times of celebration came, I felt invisible. I could not enjoy family reunions or never felt welcome there. Even in my own home, I never felt welcome. I felt out of place or on the sideline. I was like a decoration or outside of family gatherings or like a sore, a boil, when at business meetings, restaurants, school, or community events. It was like I wasn't there. If they did see me, they avoided me. My voice was heard as a screech of *mutaniak* as my pain seemed to scream out, but nobody heard or saw my pain. They avoided me or shunned me. Father, I have chosen to forgive (_____) and all of my family and all others who contributed to this painful, unwelcome plight that I found myself in. I take this pain from my heart, and I turn it over to Jesus on the cross, and I choose to never call it back.

Invisibility made people think that I didn't need to be heard or to be given a "thank you," that I didn't need to hear any words of encouragement at any time, or that I didn't need to be appreciated as a spouse, parent, supporter/provider. I was like dirt, and I felt like dirt. This caused a pain in me that has forced me to seek out my needs to be filled in others, yet it even drove them further away. At times it made me invisible even to myself. All I could feel was my pain. All I could sense was loss, no mate there, even if they slept beside me in bed; I wasn't there for them and they weren't there for me. As a parent, there were always the demanding needs of the children, never a thank you, never appreciation, or an "I love you".

Nothing was noticed or good enough to be acknowledged. Nothing was said that supported me, as a child of God, or supported me as an honored member of anything. Going through this lack of support caused me such pain that I have been unable, in the past, to forgive my mate, my family, friends and acquaintances for this pain and for their part in stripping me naked of my will, my individuality, and my ability to appreciate the gifts of God and be thankful for all the blessings I do have. This was all stripped from me under this invisibility. I turn over to Jesus this pain and this degrading humiliation. I thank You, God, for the restoration and infilling that You have given me, that You are supporting me and allowing me to change and see things differently, and to be free.

Father, invisibility has made me feel excluded from my mate, from their activities, their thoughts, from their hopes and plans, even their purpose and desires. At times I have even felt disconnected from You and Your involvement in my life. I take the effects of this pain and turn them over. The pain of not being involved, that cut off feeling as though I was a smell or a mess in the corner, not being an active part of (_____)'s life or being able to share their thoughts and they to share in my thoughts. Also the pain of having no hope of unity or being a part of something bigger than myself, not being a part of the plans for the future or development of the children, never part of having an overall purpose available to me. These are the pains and affects I have to turn over, and all the losses that came with them. I know that only in Jesus can they be restored. I forgive (_____) and everyone who has been involved in increasing these feelings of exclusion and disconnect. I choose to set them free from my distress.

As time progressed, I felt that I wasn't being fed as an individual member of my family or my marriage but like a dog, kept outside away from everything, given the scraps or whatever was left over; never the newness or freshness, never the uplifting. People did not seek me out. I was not sought for things that counted: only the menial tasks of life, but not the things that counted or were considered important in someone else's eyes. No one could empathize with my pain of being invisible. Because of that, no one could appreciate the distance that Satan and invisibility had put between me and my mate, or me and my family, or me and my desires, or even me and my God, my Father in heaven. They were things that were passed over or wiped away.

This put a false identity of who I was. I allowed myself to wither as a person, became a shell, used up and thrown away and forgotten. I choose to forgive myself for accepting these pains. I choose to forgive (_____) and my family, and I do. I choose to release them and myself for assisting in invisibility's hurt in these matters. And I turn over all that pain to Jesus on the cross and I thank you Father that I may see myself as your son/daughter.

My mate (_____), family and friends were encouraged by this cloak of invisibility to make assumptions about me, to take advantage of me, to be ungrateful to me, to treat me like a bad odor, or a mist on the mirror; who earned nothing and deserved nothing. I accepted this or enabled them because I had unforgiveness, this uselessness, and this hopelessness. I had let this invisibility oppress me and to believe that that is all I could ever be. I would look in the mirror and just see the mist, not a person. I wouldn't see a person who had a calling or anointing from God. I let my resentment grow into that mist, and to those who saw me as that mist. I let that pain fester, and the sore points that came around it would fester.

That enabled invisibility to sour my life, sour my heart, and sour my thinking, so that all that came out of me was sour. I wasn't speaking the words of love into others; I couldn't sow the seed of love into others because I had been so drained. I missed opportunities to sow good into others and to reap a harvest. I realize that this cloak of invisibility formed the assumptions that were made about me. As for the people I was looking to as friends, or as support, I couldn't receive them because I couldn't sow the seed of love; I was like mist having nothing behind it.

I had nothing to give. I couldn't sow into building up my self-worth so I could have taken advantage of open-door opportunities. There were assumptions and the pain of feeling like nothing prevented me. I couldn't even talk to myself in the mirror because there was nothing there. I choose to forgive myself, (_____), my family, my friends, my acquaintances for allowing invisibility and encouraging invisibility to see me as this mist. I turn over these false images, these assumptions and pains over to Jesus on the cross.

Father, I felt taken advantage of at every turn as though I was a workhorse, and given duties, responsibilities and chores. It was like being given moldy straw to eat because I wasn't worthy of the good stuff. I wasn't worthy of the bread of life. My energy was drained from me, as well as my enthusiasm, my integrity, and my purpose. Everything was taken from me and broken to pieces. I was never looked upon as though anything that I had as a demand or a need, or anything that I gave in service had any value. All I did and was, went without gratitude.

Love was denied; praise was denied; recognition of pain was even denied. Even a hug that would show an acknowledgement that I was there was denied. Invisibility made me a clog in everyone's eyes including my own. I have chosen to forgive myself and everyone for these pains. I have chosen to release this mist, this false image of being just a workhorse, a receiver of duty and responsibility. I have released this identity to Jesus of being just a pawn. I forgive myself and everyone for these pains.

The cloak of invisibility caused others to be uncommunicative. I was expected to read their mind. I was to know what their wants were, and they wouldn't have to talk to me. They wouldn't tell me what their wants were, what their desires were, or what their needs were, but I was expected to know them and fill them and be the source of their happiness. These unspoken expectations that I couldn't meet caused (_____) and family to resent me. They resented any demands I had that resembled my needs, wants, and suggestions.

They rejected my involvement in anything. Even my presence was rejected, sensing their feeling of "why do you have to come along?" I kept accepting this degradation. By enabling my pain, I have been increasing my demands on those around me to try to fill my needs, which only strengthened invisibility's hold over my life, (_____)'s life, my family's life, my friend's life, and my in-law's life. All those around me are being affected by the strengthening of this invisibility.

I ask for forgiveness, and I choose to forgive everyone who has enabled this invisibility, to drain me, to frustrate me. These pains have prevented them from hearing me; if I am not screaming in front of their face, then I don't exist. I take this pain and every aspect that unforgiveness has created, and I turn it over to Jesus on the cross along with all the barbs, put downs, and misunderstandings they have created.

Invisibility labeled me a "blaming tag." I felt that everything that went wrong in the family, in the job or business, in (_____)'s life, and in the church was my fault. Anything that went wrong, people were looking to blame me; somehow it all became my fault. I was the one punished for their mistakes and mine. I was the one being condemned and negated. Things did not prosper, and I couldn't bring prosperity to others because I didn't have anything to give. When things turned out right, they took all the credit, reward, and praise.

This made me feel even more deprived, useless, invisible, and it was all my fault. I choose to forgive myself for all the tags of blame that have hurt my heart and even destroyed my ability to love. I choose to forgive all who stole myself, my work, and my talent, and claimed credit for my successes, yet they blamed me for everything that went wrong. I do choose to forgive them and turn over the pain. I realize I am not the one on the cross, but Jesus died for me.

When I cried out for help or for love, invisibility stuffed me with rejection, loneliness, lameness, and avoidance. Every place I turned to be accepted, I found that I was rejected. When I looked for friendship, I was left alone. It was like trying to force yourself into a clique and no one knew you were there. The desire to bring pleasure into my life just brought emptiness (as do addictions) and added more and more to the emptiness and lameness, so that I couldn't move out of the situation. I started to avoid people, avoid involvement, and separate myself from the family, whether extending the hours working in the garden or extended hours hiding in the garage, or in the bedroom reading, so I didn't have to deal with the pain. I was looking for a quick fix, and simply didn't have energy to face responsibilities or create newness.

Sometimes I thought I was better off dead, or to be someplace else or even with someone else. Maybe they would recognize me. Nothing helped this pain -- not even in fantasies or daydreams. There was no help for this rejection, loneliness, emptiness, this blaming and need to seek avoidance. I choose to forgive, now, all those who never saw me as part of something, as a called or chosen person of God, those who never answered my deep cry for help. I turn over to Jesus this false identity. I reject that I am the lonely and never to be loved.

Father, when invisibility burdened me with responsibilities, labors, toil, and assignments, I was left alone with it all. I had no support from my family, my friends, or my in-laws. I couldn't see anyone coming to my aid. It seemed that my cry for help and my needs were going unmet all the time. This placed a tremendous burden on me. I felt so alone, Father, that I couldn't even perceive You being able to see me, help me or love me. This cloak of invisibility had shut You out. I let these burdens all overwhelm me. I let them be a false identity, a false sense of security, and a false purpose of continuing living, enduring this cloak of invisibility. I see that this is a choice that I should never have made. I shouldn't have taken on this false identity of being a burden bearer, with all the responsibilities towards the happiness of others and the saving of them. I choose to forgive (_____) and all those who placed all these burdens and labors and tasks and toils and assignments upon me. I realize, in reality, they were avoiding me, just like I was, and not turning things over to Jesus. I give back this shawl of false responsibilities to Jesus and I accept Jesus as my Burden-bearer, who is responsible for carrying, destroying and removing all yokes. I release myself to Jesus, since He's the only One who can do this.

Invisibility put a crawl over me like you put a sheet over things when you close up a house or a cabin for the winter. You don't see what is underneath, whether it has value. (_____) didn't acknowledge, protect or cherish me the way I longed for. I was put in cold storage while (_____), his/her family, friends seemed to take #1 priority in his/her life.

I was only allowed to be shown off like a toy for relatives, in-laws and friends, and not appreciated as a person, an adult, or a parent. I choose to forgive (_____) and all those who enforced invisibility's cruel crawl over me. I turn over that crawl and all the pain, regrets, dreads, and the coldness that it has caused me. I turn this over to Jesus on the cross because I don't see life at the epitome of abundance while in the depths of the cold storage.

Father, invisibility made my marriage a joke. As two we could not become one. It was never "we", "us", or even "our" in all the things of the marriage. It was always "me", "myself" and "I" to my mate. I was just assumed to be the babysitter, the cook, the housekeeper, or the provider, or sex-toy, not the helpmeet. There was no mate growing in unity. This invisibility has taken away my heart to be part of my mate, or being part of giving, loving and supporting. As a member of my mate's family I was never accepted; I was never spoken over as accepted; never laid hands on and blessed as a member of their family; never blessed with prosperity, peace or belonging. I felt the sting of being a focal point for these in-laws. When they released hostility towards me, I felt it. Words didn't have to be said, but I felt it. It cut like many knives through the air, yet they chose to never see me as part of my mate. And, I never had my mate's, (_____)'s backing or support in dealing with my in-laws because I was invisible. This cloak had made me not a person. This made me resort to living a lie, role-playing, and event games to play in order to appease and reduce the hostilities of rejection. I was judged as inadequate, inferior, as not worthy to carry my name (or the family name?). It was she/he, it, her/him, or to get attention from afar it was "Hello?" And in writing of my name, it was never spelled right. It was like I never had a name or it was never important in their eyes. I was demeaned for having feelings, or being sensitive about the way I was being treated. If I treated them like that, they would have sharply corrected me and held a grudge against me. Yet they felt it was okay to treat me like that, and sow this hatred into me. No independent thought was permitted from me.

Whatever the in-laws thought or decided, seemed to be the law, for my life, my mate's, my family and my home. What I had to say meant nothing. When I tried to pursue with my suggestions, or give advice, I got no recognition; I felt ignored, condemned, and as though I was the donkey that had just had it's tail pinned to its nose. I was the joke to them everywhere; at the gatherings, business meetings, and whenever I came near them. And, Father, whenever I tried to tell my distress to (_____), I was told the typical cliché of "Oh, I'm not responsible for your happiness!" which in itself is true, but a mate is indeed responsible for my sadness and my lack of support, and his/her lack of acceptance of me as a whole person. I choose to forgive (_____) and my in-laws for making my marriage a joke, and not allowing us to be as one, part of one another's lives, and partnered for life. I turn the pain of not having the "we", "us" or "our" in our relationship. It has dominated and diminished our marriage in Jesus. I turn over the pain of no blessings and no acceptance by my in-laws, and I accept my new family in Jesus.

Father, invisibility has boxed me in with the aid of unforgiveness and its thirty-three tormentors. I have been unable to move past this pain in order to grow in Jesus, to expand and use the talents that You have given me. I have been unable to see the horizons of possibilities because of this being boxed in by invisibility. I thank You, Father for renewing in me Your grace of forgiveness, Your purpose for my life, Your plans, Your destiny, and most of all, Your love. I forgive (_____) and all those who tried to keep me boxed in unforgiveness that caused these the tormentors to be activated in my life. I call back what they have stolen from me and I do chose to walk in forgiveness and love.

Having been invisible to others and often to myself, Father, I have accepted the pain of being pushed into accepting exaggeration against myself from others that is a mocking. It is very painful to have every suggestion, thought or idea brushed away as though it were a pesky fly, and even when what I said does eventually prove to be correct, nothing is said to verify it, or to give credit. I may have even felt condemnation for having suggested it. When words have been given to me by You, or by the Holy Spirit and I speak them out, I feel a resentment for it, and for even being in their presence. Father, I choose to forgive all those who have exaggerated the affects of invisibility against me, and I turn this pain over to Jesus on the cross, and never to be called back.

The wraps of invisibility have attacked in extremes, twisting and denial. When I have tried to fight the effects of this invisibility on my own, backlash has come upon me. My peace, happiness, and joy, anything that would be 'mine' from anything that I've done, has been stolen. My words of concern have been pushed away in every extreme possible way and I am made to look foolish and mocked because they won't listen to what I am saying, like I am talking in a foreign language to them and they laugh at it. They have twisted my words to be unrecognizable to what I really said. These words are being blocked with denial, "I've never heard that before", or "you've never said that". This has caused a hope for normality to be lost. I call that normality back. I call back all that invisibility has stolen, with its extremes, twisting and denial. Therefore, I turn over to Jesus all the loss, all the affects that invisibility has caused with its extremes, twisting, and denial, blockage, backlash, and pain. I turn this all over to Jesus, on the cross, and I forgive (_____) and all those who have encouraged it all.

In conclusion, I thank You Father, that this cloak of invisibility is taken from me and given to Jesus. I give You thanks that I am free to receive the coat of righteousness and Your armor as my defense and gifts. I thank You that I am forgiven, that I can forgive myself, my mate (_____), my family, my in-laws, and my friends, for this cloak of invisibility that was put upon me, and that You would touch them with Your grace of forgiveness to be able to forgive me for all that I did that enabled or promoted the attacks from this cloak of invisibility or its attachments to them, anything I have done that pushed them further into invisibility in my eyes or in other's. I pray for their release from it and all the affects of invisibility on them. I bless (_____), my family and in-laws and friends, my church and even my country with the peace and the joy of Jesus, and that they may all come to love You, Father, to the fullest. I pray that all power, glory and honor be Yours for ever and ever, in Jesus name. Amen and amen!

There is much that the Holy Spirit has inspired us to understand, yet we are only able to scratch the surface in this teaching. We hope that the release will be understood. Take into account or comprehend what the cloak of invisibility has stolen. Are you able to receive the full blessing of being a whole person, being seen? Are you willing to take that on and not let it be destroyed again? It is a gift from God to be appreciated. God bless you in your new freedom in marital harmony, in Jesus' name, amen.

CHAPTER 19

Get The Best Father Ever

Following are Pastor Gerald Budinski's notes for his sermon on this appropriate topic for this book. It will enable us to turn our hearts away from the father of lies and hate to the Father of truth and love...

We live in a world wrapped up in distress, fears, worries, losses, hatred, bitterness, and unforgiveness. Have you ever wondered why?

For every effect in our life, there is a cause. And for everything you sow, there is a harvest. Therefore, we can say that we've seen the effects in our lives because we've sown the bad words or actions that caused them. Our excuses abound.

"It's not my fault."

"It's not my fault," is a lie, but it is also the *biggest* source of problems that we have on earth today. It is the law of stupidity put in motion, and loosed without restraint. It establishes the blame game. "Who can I blame for what I have done?" This is at the very heart of the statement, "It's not my fault." So it begs the question, "Well, whose fault is it then?" And once the blame game is established, the worst father is released to block our communication with the Father of truth.

Everyone loves the father of lies because he always agrees with us. "It's not your fault, it's God's," because He allowed that to involve you or to do that to you.

"It's not my fault," is the calling bell for Satan to fill our bottle full of fears so that every discomfort with which he torments us results in us sucking from the bottle of fears. And out of the bottle of fears also comes: doubt, shame, guilt, anxiety, torment, pain, poverty, anger-rage, and unforgiveness.

Now, because "It's not my fault," connects us in consequence to the father of lies, we stay stuck in not being able to confess our sins in truth and faith; therefore, we can't forgive or be forgiven. This reactivates the blame game to act on the next level.

The next level is an attitude change that manifests in three ways: whininess, sympathy seeking, and addictions. The attitude is changed to: "I don't care about you, but I want you to care about me and only me." The "someone has judged me wrong" song is sung over and over.

"It's not my fault," is causing a self-centeredness that produces rejection, and as the amount of rejection grows, the level of whininess increases, the level of complaining that we produce increases our demands on others. The consumption of their time, their energy and their resources also comes to the forefront.

"It's not my fault," then allows Satan to plant the thoughts of "if" so that doubt brings blaming of God for every wrong thing…

> "If God loved me, I wouldn't have lost that job."
> "If God didn't favor others so much, I would be rich, famous, married, and popular."
> "If God loved me, I would be healed by now."
> "If God loved me, He would make my wife obey me."
> "If God loved me, He would make everyone respect me."

The "if" is a type of blaming that claims, "Nothing is my fault, it's because God doesn't have my best interest at heart. Therefore, my wrong attitudes are fully justified. And that means I am no longer responsible for anything because God is stopping my success, career, and prosperity that I deserve."

The "if" causes one to cry in pain or cry in one's beer because one's paradigm is never met, day after day. "God will have to change His ways or I will just have to die in sadness and regrets." Then the following statement rules the logic center of the brain: "If only God loved me like the love He shows to others."

"It's too much work."

The second cause is, "It's too much work that God wants me to do. He expects me to pray for everything, praise Him, worship Him, be thankful, love others, meditate on Him and His Word, read and learn His Word, go to church, eat right, pay off all my debts, be cheerful and be an example to others. This is just too much work; I have no time to be me, to enjoy the good things of this world or even to experience new things. God just expects too much out of me."

The, "It's too much work," produces the "I can't" logic and reasoning. It's the cause of most of all wrong choices that we make in our lives.

If your heart, mind and will cannot agree to choose our Father and His ways of love, then we choose by default the wrong father and we live life by our own self-induced errors and choices. When we choose to fight our Father, we choose to enslave ourselves with too much work and too little pay or too much wrong results.

The "It's too much work," creates self-worship and multiple types of idol worship that breaks the first and second commandments. Idol worship will *always* cause us to walk in the flesh, speak in the flesh. We have *no* ability, *no* strength and *no* authority to fight Satan while we are moving in the flesh and doing things in accordance to the flesh.

The "It's too much work," creates a complaining attitude that builds because of resentment, bitterness and strife. You live in the turmoil of Satan's claws so that you lose all peace, joy, hope, love and faith.

"I don't have enough."

The third cause is, "I don't have enough." It enforces the "I can't," from "It's too much work." It also justifies squandering, wastage, loss, theft, dryness, hoarding, rot, erosion, misuse, and stinginess. One submits to the control of poverty and destruction in *every area* in one's life. "I don't have enough," means that Satan's get systems are being employed and not the Father's give or love system.

Not only does, "I don't have enough," trap you into accepting Satan as your father but also it causes you to reject and defy every way that the Father has opened to bless you into over two hundred blessings found in the Bible. It makes you try to defy the laws of sowing and reaping.

"I don't have enough so I can't give."
"I don't have enough so I can't tithe."
"I don't have enough so I don't have an offering."
"I don't have enough so I can't plant a garden."
"I don't have enough so I can't start a business."
"I don't have enough so I can't get ahead."
"I don't have enough so I can't get established.
"I don't have enough so it's no use trying."
"I don't have enough so God won't accept me."

These are the excuses that burn up the harvest you should've had so that you live in need, want, and the longing emptiness that Satan's kingdom produces for his children.

Until you deal with the "I don't have enough," statements that you made in your life, you'll see prosperity, belonging and purpose continually stolen from you. And your choice is always the worst father that one can have.

"Everybody else is doing it."

The fourth cause of choosing the wrong father is "Everybody else is doing it." From very young, we compare ourselves as to how good we are by the standard of looking at others. We learn from what everybody else is doing. We absorb their fears, their values and attitudes. And we absorb what makes the "myself" different from the "themselves."

It's when peer values and acceptance are learned, however, that parental values are corrupted. Our need to belong becomes so strong that any rejection caused by God's right or wrong principles means that God's principles get compromised. And it is at this point, that parental values are devalued. Satan now steps in as the *sole* evaluation of what is right or wrong. All the lessons of history are lost or stolen. Being accepted by friends and Satan becomes more important than anything else in one's life.

The "Everyone else is doing it," takes over as the guide to right and wrong, good or bad, up or down, and it establishes the feel good principles of judging ourselves and our activities. This is what creates the situation of the blind leading the blind into Satan being the best father. This is because he puts no restraints on the acceptable level of corruption. Everything one wishes for is *ho! ho! ho!* This means that every sin is good to do, or everything is just fine.

The "Everyone else is doing it," creates the strongest bond to Satan as father because it makes us agree to shut down the moral, logic, reasoning, and judgmental systems or areas of our brain. They function at eight to ten per cent of their capacity because of the bonding.

Another important bonding to Satan is the "feel good" principle. It's not a question of what God say to do, but what feels good, the warning God gives in Proverbs 16:25 that the way that seems or feels right ends in death.

"If it feels good, do it!"

This fifth cause for claiming the wrong father is that Satan advocates "If it feels good, do it," and the emotional evolution in satisfying *the emptiness that the soul feels when it is cut off from God, the Father and Jesus.* This establishes the marriages to demons, acceptance of evil traditions and the defending of all the doctrines of demons. The heart of our soul is then put into chaos and pain so it can hold neither peace nor joy. Then come the addictions to sex, drugs, food, booze, evil, horrors, gossip, lying, and such. The "If it feels good, do it," principle causes us to look for fleshly answers to spiritual problems.

This never works because we have become so accepting of everything that Satan says that we allow Satan to guide us deeper and deeper into a pit since we chose him as the father of, "If it feels good, do it." And as Satan has become a chosen father, he puts an iron grip upon us to reject all truth in favor of his lies.

"The end justifies the means."

The sixth cause for claiming the wrong father is the principle of "The end justifies the means." This principle teaches you to justify all errors, sins, wrong choices and such if you win in the end. This closes one's acceptance of justice and establishes fairness as the justifier. One goes whining to the unjust judge for fairness in matters. Satan is the unjust judge that cannot walk in righteousness, mercy or love. Those who seek him as father are burdened, shamed, and made guilty by the unfair judge of fairness.

Once these six causes are established, you are the child of the devil, bound up as fodder for destruction and living cursed lives that give no hope, purpose, peace, joy, or freedom. The father of lies and carrier of death now has a legal claim over your soul and the rest of your physical life. And to reward you for choosing him, Satan gives you sickness, loss, failure, poverty, and guilt.

It is important to understand how Satan has turned the whole world upside-down in order to establish himself as god and father to the world. Therefore the world says, "the father of lies always knows best."

But we have a choice. We can learn to be like our Father Love. We don't have to stay under Satan's yoke and bindings. We can answer the best Father's call and come to know and be like Jesus

Now compare the best with the worst:

Our Heavenly Father is Love, whereas Satan is hate.
Our Heavenly Father is kind, whereas Satan is cruelty.

Our Heavenly Father is gentle, whereas Satan is harsh.

Our Heavenly Father is truth, whereas Satan is a liar.

Our Heavenly Father is life whereas Satan is death.

Our Heavenly Father is patient, whereas Satan is impatient.

Our Heavenly Father is Creator, whereas Satan is destroyer.

Our Heavenly Father is revealer, whereas Satan is deceiver.

Our Heavenly Father is Provider.	Satan is taker.
Our Heavenly Father is giver.	Satan is getter.
Our Heavenly Father is tolerant.	Satan is intolerant.
Our Heavenly Father is light.	Satan is darkness.
Our Heavenly Father is Defender.	Satan is betrayer.
Our Heavenly Father is "Prosperer."	Satan is scammer.
Our Heavenly Father is honorable.	Satan is dishonorable.
Our Father is covenant keeper.	Satan is entrapper.
Our Heavenly Father is Establisher.	Satan is "underminer."
Our Heavenly Father is a Shield.	Satan is attacker.
Our Heavenly Father is a "Blesser."	Satan is curser.
Our Heavenly Father is worthy.	Satan is unworthy.
Our Heavenly Father is Refiner.	Satan is polluter.
Our Heavenly Father is Definer.	Satan is legalist.
Our Heavenly Father is Purifier.	Satan is corrupter.
Our Heavenly Father is Lifter.	Satan is oppressor.

We can change and grow strong, wise and knowledgeable in Father Love when we seek to know Him and think like He does. Or we can grow weak, sour, and stupid when we reject Father Love in favor of the father of lies. Know the Eternal God and His ways and have a life of peace, joy, prosperity, and confidence. Or stay stuck in Satan's pit and know hopelessness, futility, and barrenness that tax ninety-nine per cent of your potential and life so that he can torture you with pain.

If we don't feed ourselves on the Word of truth, our soul starves and Satan overpowers us and steals our blessings. Don't be *deceived*; the days are short and Satan is pouring on the pressure. Choose the best

Father and His ways; choose Jesus as your Guide into a joyous, secure, and abundant life.

We bless you with the wisdom to wisely choose lives of joy, in Jesus' name, amen.

CHAPTER 20

No Spiritual Warfare—
No Spiritual Welfare

While attendance at Christian churches is dwindling, the ranks of witches and Satanists are burgeoning. The Christian world has no idea of the power of these evil forces, an army of diligent warriors who believe more strongly in their cause than those whose power source is much greater than Satan's.

It's pitiful. And Satanists and witches are boasting of their power and laughing at the impotence of the Christians. These people who have tapped into the forces of evil in many cases know thousands of Bible verses. They know the Bible better than those who are supposed to read and live by it.

One of our bloggers asked how do witches know so much about what believers are supposed to be doing and the believers seem so devoid of understanding?"

A strong believer who came out of this darkness answered her that witches have books of instructions they read and reread to get the most out of what is said. She said that most Christians don't even know where their Bible is, let alone find anything in it. She pointed out that a witch studies to know who they are and what they can become, while Christians can't even tell the difference between lord and Jesus.

Another enlightened believer added that when witches enters the third level they start to learn the tomes of cursing, and why certain things must be stopped in believers in order to bring about the kingdom of Satan as universal dominance. She said that many witches have learned thousand of scriptures over the years while Christians can spend weeks trying to find their Bible. Witches are also taught the power of the word and words we speak, she related. Christians seem to only want to learn the F--- word. She wondered why they don't even want to know that the Lord is referring to the demon quagmire.

With all the witchcraft movies seducing young and old, and with Satan putting on the pressure because he has shortened his time (Rev. 12:12), the forces of evil are gaining ground outside and inside the church. Christian organizations and parents can't see the harm in the witchcraft craze in books and movies affecting their children, so supposedly Christian youth camps introduce activities based on these movies, films that introduce children to witchcraft. Halloween is celebrated among Christians, and no harm is seen in it.

Wasn't Good Supposed to Overcome Evil?

Wasn't good supposed to overcome evil? These days evil is overcoming good. These partners of evil have tomes of curses aimed at Christians. They regularly sacrifice babies to enforce their powerful curses, while Christians say things like, "Curses? Oh come on, now. We have Jesus. We can't be affected by curses." All the while they refuse to use Jesus' blood in communion to break off the devastating effect of these curses.

A dangerous paradox is allowing Satan to get an upper hand that he was not supposed to get. God tells believers in His Word to know the schemes of the devil, but most will discount the influence of demons on Christians. What is even more shocking is that those who work for the devil, the witches and warlocks, know much more about the plans God has for believers than believers know about the plans of the devil. Witches have studied and meditated on thousands of Bible passages to know how to wound Christians with their own sword. Still, ignorant Christians scoff at the power evil wields.

Years ago we got a peek of some satanic tomes of curses. The surprising thing is that these dwellers in darkness know more of what the people of the light are supposed to be doing than the Christians themselves! And witches use the energy and light of the increasingly nonchalant Christians for themselves to make their spells, hexes, and incantations more powerful.

Where do you stand in this battle of the last days? And are you standing? Or are you like most defenseless Christians, strewn all over the battlefield, in some cases down but not even realizing that you have been beaten?

In case you don't know, the evil forces have the upper hand. The church is asleep, and even when its members were awake, they didn't know their power in Jesus because they didn't know their identity in Him. The witches and Satanists are awake and zealous for their evil cause, while a neither hot nor cold church languishes nonchalantly into a deep sleep, not even concerned about being vomited out of Jesus' mouth (Rev. 3:15-16).

So how can the hearts of God's children be turned to their Father Love when they are under attack from the evil side, wounded and/or shell-shocked? In many cases clouds of dullness and domes of darkness make them oblivious to their condition. Church, it's time we wake up and become aware of the enemy's tactics.

That's biblical. God tells us not to be ignorant of the devil's schemes (2 Cor. 2:11), yet most Christians willingly are. While the deceived Christian world is keeping feasts based in paganism and ignoring God's commanded days in the Bible, our enemies are keeping the same pagan feasts, often in sexual revelry and human sacrifice, cursing Christians who have no idea they are being cursed. In fact, Christians don't care.

You don't think the evil side is winning? Former practitioners of the dark arts on our blog got tired of the lies and traditions in the churches, so they went into the camp of darkness. They are now powerful believers in Jesus with great insight from the Holy Spirit aided by having engaged in the practices they now expose.

One such believer on our blog explained that what pushes women out of the churches and into witchcraft is the number of spells of seduction, the lack of leadership, the amount of lies and lying that they have to put up with, the amount of hypocrisy that pastors will speak out in order to justify disobeying God in order to keep wrong traditions, and the doctrines of demons that have been incorporated into church belief. She said that if you have to worship Satan in the churches, you feel more comfortable worshipping him directly through witchcraft.

Our Father desires worship in spirit and truth (John 4:24). It's time we learned how to gain the victory over our enemy and reach the heart of our Father.

CHAPTER 21

We Need Peace!

We all need peace. But we don't find it in the world. And sadly, we don't even find it in most believers today.

The first book I read after accepting Jesus was by a famous evangelist who was born a few miles away from my home, *Peace with God*, by Billy Graham. I began to experience peace with my Father through Jesus Christ His Son. I had no idea, however, what plans Satan had to try to destroy my peace. And he is doing a number on many Christians today, destroying their peace.

We can't turn our hearts to Father Love except through our acceptance of and relationship with Jesus. He is the Door to the Father. He gives us His peace by reconciling us to the Father. Jesus told us that the world could not bring us peace, but we believers have allowed the world around us to invade us and rob us of our peace.

Job prophesied it. His seven sons prefigured seven years of sorrow that would precede what his daughters symbolized, the Tribulation, the Great Tribulation, and the wrath of God.

Most Christians know about Job's trials and how terribly he suffered. Those troubles prophesied the challenges believers are facing in these last days. Job's words in Job 3: 13 are especially significant in relation to the lack of peace in this end time: "For now I would have lain down and been quiet; I would have slept then, I would have been at rest."

Job is saying what many Christians are saying in this time of tribulation we are living in today: "When the good times with God ended, why don't we just fall asleep and have peace and quiet awaiting the call of Jesus at His return. With all these spiritual and financial trials, why can't we just die and go to heaven?" The last days' scenario is one of ever-increasing troubles from which there seems to be no rest, no quiet time to recuperate and regain strength.

Job wanted God to take him out of his troubles, even if it meant death. Some have said that Job had a thousand boils. They symbolized the number of major trials most believers face in their lives, trials that are multiplying in these last days. Job's words prophesied that Christians would cry out, "Just let me go to heaven, God. When will the rapture come to get us out of this mess? We see sorrows and confusion upon sorrows and confusion so that we see no rest for our brains. Where is Your wisdom and Your love for us now?"

Believers are plagued with problems, problems of health, marriage, finances, jobs and business, problems from betrayers and from tares within the church. False gods and addictions rob Christians of sleep. Integrity and loyalty are lacking. More and more believers, including pastors, burn out. Peace is absent.

It seems the time is isn't there to escape from the problems God's way. The challenges keep coming faster and harder. The church sees its work assignment continue to increase while funding and time seemed stretched beyond limits. We feel overwhelmed.

We want to let peace into our hearts, but most are not succeeding.

Where is peace? How do we find it in these turbulent times?

Jesus asked if he would find faith on the earth among His people in these last days (Luke 18:8). Faith works hand-in-hand with love, yet He said that the love of many would grow cold (Mat. 24:12). God prophesied that pastors and others who would try to heal the brokenness of the believers superficially would proclaim, " Peace, peace, But there is no peace" (Jer. 6:14).

Indeed, where is peace? Where has the peace of the believers gone? Why are they not able to let peace into their hearts? Receiving the answer requires that we ask and answer another important question: "What is peace?"

What Is Peace?

One of our radio listeners asked us that very question. While that is an excellent question, it reminds us of the question the Roman governor asked at Jesus' trial: "What is truth?" Truth was so absent that he had to ask the question. And peace is so absent in our society, even among Christians, that we have to ask the question.

The answer is actually quite simple, but to know what peace is, you must have it in yourself or see it in others. It is a gift from Jesus and part of the fruit of the Spirit. But we must be willing to receive it into our hearts.

Peace is simply the absence of conflict or turmoil among people or in ourselves. John 14:27 says that Jesus has given His peace to us, His disciples. That inner peace is part of the fruit of the Spirit in Galatians 5:22.

That peace, however, resides in our spirits, which have been made perfect by the blood of Jesus. Whether it is transmitted to our souls, or our hearts, minds, and wills, depends on us. Jesus warned us, saying, "Do not let your heart be troubled, nor let it be fearful" (John 14:27).

Jesus promised us an abundant life of peace in John 10:10, but we have our part to play. Jesus said that the thief Satan would try to come to steal our peace. Thoughts and words of fear allow Satan to steal our peace so that it's not able to reside in our souls and be a function of our life.

God tells us to be anxious or fearful for nothing (Phil. 4:6). Paul commands us in Philippians 4 to rejoice always and never to pray in fear but with a spirit of thanksgiving, thinking thankful thoughts and expressing thanksgiving to God as we pray. In that way the peace of God that passes all understanding will guard our hearts and minds as we stay fixed on Jesus.

When Paul says that the peace of Jesus passes our comprehension, he means that peace is something we can understand only when we see it in others or ourselves. We can even see it by looking at the animals when they are at peace or when they are disturbed.

The peace of Jesus does indeed protect our hearts and minds from the turmoil around us. Jesus was at peace amid a storm, and when he awoke, he spoke to the storm. He spoke peace to the storm. He told us how we could speak to the mountains or problems in our life rather than speaking about them. We could speak to the mountain and cause it to be cast into the sea.

Speaking God's Word into our circumstances allows us to have Jesus' peace in our hearts. Being afraid of the storm that swirls around us in speaking out words of fear robs us of our peace.

Isaiah 26:12 gives us a key to understanding peace and causing it to be established in our hearts: "[Jesus], You will establish peace for us, since You have also performed for us all our works."

As with peace, righteousness is a gift from Jesus, and they work together. Depending on our own strength causes a lack of peace. Trusting in Jesus and His righteousness in us brings peace. We are not performing the works. He is.

Peace Amid the Storm?

Isaiah 54:11 speaks of people who allow themselves to be "storm-tossed," having no comfort as they are hit by the waves of bad circumstances around them.

Jesus offers the solution in verse 14: "In righteousness you will be established; You will be far from oppression, for you will not fear; and from terror, for it will not come near you."

In other words, we confess our sins to our Father and forgive ourselves, accepting Jesus' blood to erase our sins. We accept His righteousness as a gift (2 Cor. 5:17, 20-21). He took our sins and gave us as a replacement His righteousness. As we accept that truth in our hearts, we also receive His peace.

Isaiah 32:17 emphasizes this truth: "And the work of righteousness will be peace, and the service of righteousness, quietness and confidence forever."

The English word *peace* is only a small part of the meaning of the Hebrew word *shalom*. We want to end this message with a blessing from some powerful Hebrew words, including *shalom*, but we must first understand those words.

Since most Christians read much of the New Testament, you have probably noticed how often Paul blesses his readers with grace and peace. And a connection does exist between the two. Isaiah 26:12 explains that connection, and it bears repeating, from the NIV: "[Jesus], you establish peace for us; all that we have accomplished you have done for us."

Most Christians don't understand that grace is an empowerment to do what Jesus calls us to do. In essence, it's Him in us doing the good works. When we understand that Jesus in us is the Grace or supernatural ability doing the works through us, we have peace.

Jeremiah 17 speaks of the man who trusts in himself and "makes flesh his strength" (Jer. 17:5). The description of him being "like a bush in the desert" (verse 6) is not a picture of peace.

Notice how God describes the one who trusts in Jesus and allows Him to do the works rather than relying on his own strength: "Blessed is the man who trusts in [Jesus] and whose trust is [Jesus]. For he will be like a tree planted by the water, that extends its roots by a stream and will not fear when heat comes; but it's leaves will be green, and it will not be anxious in a year of drought nor cease to yield fruit" (Jer. 17:7-8).

Having no fear or anxiety keeps Satan from stealing the peace of Jesus from this man. He lives the abundant life of peace Jesus promised (John 14:27; John 10:10).

Sadly, however, since September 11, 2001, North American Christians have allowed fear to overwhelm them. They speak words of fear, even in their prayers. God doesn't receive words of fear, since He is Love. So Satan is hearing and answering in a bad way many of the prayers of these fearful saints. Those prayers affect those Christians these saints are praying for unless they are rejected and broken off. Fear is paralyzing the saints so the saints can't go "marching in" as the song says, to the Kingdom of Love.

Fear is also robbing the believers of their peace.

A Divided Heart Cannot Turn
Itself to the Father's Heart

A heart of fear can't be turned to the heart of Father Love. A heart of fear is far from the Father's heart of love. And a heart of fear is often a divided heart.

Zebulun's warriors "helped David with an undivided heart" (1 Chron. 12:33). David also wanted an undivided heart focused on Jesus (Ps. 86:11). Paul encouraged the saints to do whatever was necessary to secure "undistracted devotion to [Jesus]" (1 Cor. 7:35).

God prophesied that in the end time men will be lovers of pleasure and money, having only an outward appearance of piety but far from the Father's heart of love (2 Tim. 3:1-6). Paul warned of the danger of eating at God's table and the table of demons at the same time (1 Cor. 10:21). Such a compromise will eventually rip a believer apart.

Elijah chided those who hesitated between two opinions (1 Kings 18:21). How can we stay together in peace and in one piece if we're leaning in two opposite directions? Joshua challenged the believers in his day, but his challenge remains for us today: "…choose for yourselves today whom you will serve… but as for me and my house, we will serve [Jesus]" (Josh. 24:15).

Peace has been defined as the absence of conflict. So why would we introduce conflict where it doesn't exist? A battle already exists in our minds between the Holy Spirit in us and the flesh (Gal. 5:17). So why invite in lusts that "wage war against the soul" (1Pet. 2:11)?

A number of factors can destroy our peace. Unforgiveness brings in numerous demonic tormentors that make peace impossible. And the many facets of lust, fifty-six in all, open doors to every other sin. Sin robs us of our peace.

So why do end-time believers give up their peace so readily? For many, it's because they do three things that open the door to lust. They engage in fantasy desires. They wish for things and people, and they complain as Satan did that things aren't fair.

When we invite lust in, a little leaven begins to leaven the whole lump. Soon the many facets of lust will engulf our lives, corrupting our souls so as to make it impossible to receive and appreciate any of the bountiful blessings of our Father Love. Our eyes are so busy lusting after evil that we cannot see any of our Father's perfect gifts.

Lust will have replaced love in our lives, while love for God and others is the foundation of our peace. When we have a love and respect for God's laws of love, we have great peace that cannot be ruffled by people or circumstances (Ps. 119:165).

Loving and serving others is a key to peace. Our heart is thus undivided in our service to God and others. We're not spending our time thinking about ourselves and finding reasons to lose our peace.

That's why Peter encouraged us to purify our souls by loving and serving others, thus bringing joy and peace to our souls: "Since you have in obedience to the truth purified your souls for a sincere love of the brethren, fervently love one another from the heart…" (1 Pet. 1:22).

An undivided heart of love and devotion dedicated to serving God and man is a pure heart that produces peace and spreads that peace around us. Indeed, how can we be the peacemakers God calls us to be if our heart is not at peace?

A heart focused on Jesus is a heart that will be effectively turned back to the Father's heart of love. The men and women we read about in the Hebrew Scriptures didn't know the Father (John 5:37). The only knew *of* Him. Jesus came later to reveal the Father (John 1:18). But men after God's own heart like David sought Jesus with all their heart and soul, as a thirsty man yearned for water in the desert (Psalms 42 and 63). David had an undivided focus, as did Paul. They wanted to be more intimate with Jesus (Ps. 27:4; Phil. 3:8-10).

We can't get past level two of faith without focusing our eyes on Jesus and getting to know Him, especially through His Word. Our hearts can thus be turned in love to our earthly fathers and to our heavenly Father.

Paul learned the secret of living in peace no matter what the circumstance (Phil. 4:6-13). He did it by God's grace, the empowerment of Jesus in him. That's probably why he was inspired to repeatedly bless his readers, which include us today, with the grace and peace He had received from God.

A Blessing of Grace and Peace

We would also like to bless our readers with grace and peace. Before we extend that blessing to you, we should examine the concepts of grace and peace in the original Bible languages.

The most powerful word for grace, only taking a back seat to *shelam* and *shalom* as far as words of great blessing in Hebrew, is the word *chanan* in Genesis 43:29. Joseph said to his younger brother Benjamin, "May God be gracious to you, my son…" The word comes from the root meaning, "incline favor to" or "bend a favorable ear towards." It means: stoop down to show kindness to an inferior; bestow a kindness; have God's light shine on a person, exposing him or her for blessings; to beseech a favor from God for a person; ask someone to pray for you; grant a favor to; deal in favor; strength to deal favorably with another; entreat a higher authority for blessing for another; to call for mercy for yourself or another; have mercy.

While mercy is not grace, as many falsely believe, grace can include mercy. Grace includes the empowerment to get up when we fall, thanks to the mercy of God.

Other definitions include: have compassion upon; take us out of a mess we have made for ourselves; pray for another's prosperity (includes *shalom*, asking for God's grace to make them whole); pray for the wholeness of another's family; make supplication to God for another; to be called of God for a future job. He calls us first in order to disciple us. We must first learn His Word and be open to Him, to learn from Him.

When Joseph beseeched God for grace for Benjamin, he made Jesus bend His ear to fill all his needs, to be kind to him and his family, to walk in His favor in family prosperity, and that Jesus would find a job for Benjamin to do in order to please God. We need about sixty words to only partially say what Joseph said in one word, *chanan*, one of the most powerful word blessings you can give in conceptual Hebrew.

When a person cried out to God to receive back his cloak he gave as pledge, so he could be warm and sleep at night, God said, "I will hear him, for I am *gracious*" (Ex. 22:27). The word is *channuwn* or *chanun*, "to be gracious."

The multiple meanings of this word include the following: move to respond to one's need; ask God to respond to our need; call for an injustice to be corrected, and the right to ask God to correct it; have God speak into an evil or hardship; have God redeem you from a problem or a debt; have God declare His mercy on you; favor in the eyes of our accusers, creditors, or bosses; overcome human relations problems (overcome with God as well); beseech God for His justice to come into a problem; pray for God's grace that allows for *empowerment in all difficulties or problems – even a persistent sin*; to find God's blessing of faith, hope, and love bestowed on us for obeying His voice.

The most powerful word involving grace, however, is *chanan* from Genesis 43. We will use that word in giving a priestly blessing to you believers, many who will have also accepted their anointing as priests of God.

Remember that as spiritual priests or Levites we have a covenant with our God that guarantees life and peace (Mal. 2:5). Our part of that covenant is to stand in awe of the name of Jesus, relying on His power in us so that no words of fear or unrighteousness is found on our lips as we walk in His peace (Mal. 2:5-6).

One of the most powerful blessings in the Bible is contained in Numbers 6:22-26. It is no coincidence that it also contains two most powerful words of blessing in the Hebrew language, *shalom* and *chanan*, or gracious. Jesus told Moses to tell Aaron to bless Israel, the believers, with this potent blessing.

We pray that you will be able to receive these encouraging words of blessing today: "[Jesus] bless you, and keep you; [Jesus] make His face shine on you, And be gracious [*chanan*] to you; [Jesus] lift up His countenance on you, And give you peace [*shalom*]."

You have been blessed with peace. All you need to do is to receive the blessing.

One of the sure ways to allow it into our hearts to stay is to continually turn over to Jesus that which does not make for peace in our lives. We turn over problems daily at the end of the day and weekly on the eve of the Sabbath, three hours before it begins Friday evening.

The most neglected turnover of those things that cause disturbances in our lives is the new moon turnover every month, when we take stock of problems of the past that haven't been turned over to Jesus.

The Bride of Jesus is called to prepare the way for the coming of the Bridegroom. But how can we do that with all this baggage from the past?

Isaiah 57:14 tells us, "Build up, build up, prepare the way..." But how can we prepare the way. He continues, "Remove every obstacle out of the way of My people" Those obstacles include the peace blockers that keep us from being at peace in our hearts.

Peace with God began with me in the form of learning from a book by that name as a teen in 1967, after I had received Jesus at a youth crusade in my native South Carolina. Peace with God and ourselves begins the moment we receive Jesus, the King of Peace.

Turning over the old self in baptism, however, is an oft-overlooked step God requires of us in order to start on the road to complete peace in our hearts and lives. The end-time revelation of the turning over of long term peace blockers at the new moon is more of a voluntary act to see how far we want to go in receiving the peace that passes understanding.

Grace and peace to you all, in Jesus' name.

CHAPTER 22

The Messiest, Most Dangerous Divorce in History

The most dramatic divorce in history is occurring before your eyes, but the gossip columnists and the scandal-seeking rags are silent. Surprisingly, the Christian world is embracing and praising this scandalous divorce.

Is it possible? Yes.

A great falling away is being prepared as the Christian world looks on in naïve wonder, believing it's from God. God hates divorce, but He especially hates this kind of divorce, and He even prophesied it.

The disciples asked the question, "Is it better not to marry." Indeed, it appears that the Bride of Jesus will miss out on the marriage because of this divorce. It's not a marital divorce. It's a divorce of covenants and testaments. You'll be surprised when you hear about this divorce.

What divorce could cause such a massive falling away?

Divorcing the Two Testaments

It's the divorce between the Old and New Covenants and the Old and New Testaments.

Jesus never divorced them. He said we are to live by every word of God, no matter which part of the Bible we find it in (Mat. 4:4). He described the New Covenant as the same Old Covenant law, yet He expanded it to include the spirit of the law, and He prophesied that the law would be written on our hearts, far from being done away (Heb. 8:8-10; Jer. 31:31-33; Mat. 5:17-20).

This breach between the covenants is described in an interesting prophecy in Isaiah 22:9-11: "And you saw that the *breaches* in the wall of the city of David were many; and you collected the waters of the lower pool. Then you counted the houses of Jerusalem and tore down houses to fortify the wall. And you made a *reservoir between the two walls* for the waters of the old pool. But you did not depend on Him who made it, nor did you take into consideration Him who planed it long ago."

What is the reservoir between the two walls? It was a sewer made between the two walls. The two walls symbolize the two testaments, Old and New, representing the Sinai and New Covenants. In essence, this was a divorce between the two. Whereas Jesus intended that the New Covenant would cause the laws of the Sinai covenant to be written on our hearts, the lie from Satan's sewer is that never the two shall meet. There is no connection. The Old Testament is called old because men want to do away with it.

God never did away with it and never will. While the Old Covenant was replaced by the New, the principles, words, and laws of the First Testament are still the basis of the New Covenant. The Holy Spirit writes its laws on our hearts. The grace or empowerment of Jesus in us enables us to keep God's laws according to the letter and the spirit. The breach between the Old and New Testaments and between law and grace must be repaired.

Repairing the Breach

Years ago God instructed us to bring a revelation to a church that was formerly a Sabbath keeping church but had abandoned it and even abandoned the truth about healing. We were to start with that healing truth, and we were hopeful they would repent. As I drove my car home after hearing that they rejected the truth, I heard an inspired song on cassette tape, which quoted our mission statement as a church, Isaiah

58. "You are the repairer of the breach," the song lyrics intoned. I knew that was our answer.

We would begin to repair the breach in the Word, the breach in the family, and the breach between God the Father *and His children*, a breach that would be powerfully and completely repaired by a coming "Elijah." Remember that Jesus said that no one could come to the Father but through Him (John 14:6). God promised to send "Elijah" as a forerunner of Jesus' return as He promised to send John the Baptist as the "Elijah" before Jesus' first coming.

God prophesied that we would remember the law of Moses with all its statutes which Jesus commanded him at Sinai (Mal. 4:4). Then Elijah would come to "restore all things" (Mat. 11:17), and would, like John the Baptist, "turn the disobedient to the attitude of the righteous" and "prepare a people for [Jesus]," a people to marry Him.

If God calls us to remember the law of Moses with all its statutes, He is going to promptly correct the heresy of the grace revolution and repair the breach or divorce between the First and Second Testaments. The law David loved (Psalm 119) that made him a man after God's heart (Acts 13:22) is the same law that God writes on our hearts in the New Covenant.

Gospel of the Kingdom, Not the Gospel of Grace

That's why Jesus preached the gospel of the Kingdom of God and prophesied that this true gospel would be preached in all the nations before the end would come. At the same time that a great falling away would unite the universal mother church with her protesting daughters, replacing God's laws with traditions of men and causing a marriage with the man of lawlessness, not with Jesus.

All this will be because they malign and misunderstand the first three-fourths of the Bible they like to call what God never called it, the "Old" Testament. It's just as much the Word of God as the last fourth. We are among those who are starting to repair the breach, the divorce, if you will, between these two parts of the Bible and the covenants they represent.

The grace revolution is saying that the New Covenant began at the crucifixion, and that the gospels are not to be taken seriously. They say that Jesus began teaching the gospel of the Kingdom before He came into the fullness of the gospel of grace that Paul supposedly preached, which he didn't (Acts 28:30-31). So the part of the Bible we should take seriously is even less than a fourth of the Bible.

Some even said years ago that we should only live by the book of Galatians. The breach is widening. The gap must be breached, and the gospel of false grace is widening, rather than breaching it.

Christians refuse to believe the First Testament, yet Ezekiel 37 prophesies the time of Revelation 20:5, the second resurrection, which most Christians don't understand. Yet many of them that embrace this falsehood about the law being done away are doing away with their marriage with Jesus. They will rise with flesh on their bones, with life given to them again after a thousand years in the grave. They didn't divorce Jesus because they will never marry Him. They miss out on the "better resurrection" (Heb. 11:35).

Will you be deceived and fall for the great falling away beginning now? Will you receive the true Kingdom message or the false grace message?

Why Can't Jesus' Disciples Get the Kingdom Message?

Jesus spent His entire ministry teaching about the Kingdom. He realized His disciples still didn't get the message. How do we know? When He was resurrected, He was "appearing to them over a period of forty days and speaking of the things concerning the kingdom of God" (Acts 1:3).

The question they asked in Acts 1:6 showed they still didn't get it. And the church still hasn't gotten it. We preach a gospel of grace rather than the gospel of the Kingdom He prophesied some would preach at the end of time (Mat. 24:14). He knew someone would get it before the last days would come. Do you?

The disciples didn't know how to pray, so they asked Jesus for some guidelines. He started the model prayer by saying "Your *Kingdom* come. Your will be done" (Mat. 6:9). His will is expressed in His Word and in His law. He ends the model prayer by saying, "For Yours is the Kingdom and the power and the glory forever…" (Mat. 6:13).

There it is. The Kingdom is the central focus of our prayers. There is no glory in a gospel of lawless grace. Glory comes when we put the Kingdom first.

We have had to write over one hundred pages because of all the excuses. When we decide with our will to practice righteousness rather than lawlessness, there are no more excuses, only submission to the Divine Master Jesus. He wants you blessed by keeping His laws of love.

Law and grace have also been divorced. Grace in the Person of Jesus, came to bring grace and truth to enable us to keep the law He gave to Moses and to all believers. Grace empowers us to keep the law. They aren't divorced as diametrically opposites as being portrayed, but they are complementary. While it's true that the law doesn't enable us to keep its rules, Jesus does indeed make the law glorious by expanding it and giving us His own power or grace to keep it.

Only Source of End-time Protection

The government has covered up the alien phenomenon, and yet the "hosts of heaven" that God created and some that were genetically manipulated by Satan are prophesied to attack in the end time. Yet God declared the Sabbath covenant just after making the heavenly hosts as a statement to all creation that the only defense in the last days against any earthly or heavenly enemy is resting in Jesus on His Sabbath day, not Sunday.

The Christian world is going to gasp in surprise when Jesus returns and commands the world to keep the Sabbath, the new moons, and His feast days, and there will be no Christmas or Easter (Isa. 66:23;

Zech. 14:16-19). A small remnant will be keeping these and all of God's laws in the last days (Rev. 12:17; 14:12). The majority won't adopt these teachings, however true they may be.

You are blessed to know how to avoid the divorce between the Old and New Testaments and to know how to be ready to marry Jesus soon. You have the choice to accept the greatest apostasy from the truth of all time or to be part of a remnant that will escape "all these things" and "stand before the Son of man" (Luke 21:36).

Few of those who buy this book may even read this far. You have read these words, and we pray you will be blessed to believe God's Word and be abundantly blessed as the world falls apart around you. Shalom. As we near the end of writing this book, TV evangelists we love and have played in our church are falling away from truth God taught them. They are beginning to teach an extremely deceptive lawlessness, claiming it is the wonderful gospel of grace. This chapter will be short, since we have published a crucial book on this important question: *Grace Revolution? — Or Deadly Deception?* Basically virtually every excuse for not obeying God and His law is covered in the book. Avoiding this great deception will open a door for you to turn your heart to the Father of Love that gave through Jesus His laws of love and His grace to keep them.

CHAPTER 23

Hope in the Darkest Night

I'm writing this in the darkest part of the night, at about 3:30 AM. It's a dark time for me, and it reminds me how God has always been faithful to me in my dark times. He will be faithful to bring Jesus and His light to shine on this earth in its darkest of times.

God rescued me as He will this world and all you who read this. I was a slave of unforgiveness, and as the movie, *Twelve Years a Slave*, depicts, I was a slave of unforgiveness for twenty-five years and of incurable illness for twelve years. Declared to die within three hours by a doctor in Quebec City in 1986, in His mercy God allowed me to live. Slavery is no fun, but freedom is a priceless gift.

I often joked about our antebellum home in South Carolina, built in a time of slavery in 1852. I would say that we had slave quarters in the back, but there were no more slaves. That wasn't totally true. We had servants, "The Help," as the movie called them. They weren't literal slaves, but we looked on them as though they were inferior beings.

My perception changed when I was sent to France as a pastor in 1973, where I met some black people that were a lot smarter than me. The head of the church I pastored, a cult at the time, had opened "Pandora's box," as he called it, by ruling that we could now officiate at black and white marriages.

I felt rejected and inferior, having insecurity as my identity instead of Jesus, when my boss over France told me it was me who opened "Pandora's box" in France when I officiated at the marriage of two people who were not "café au lait" or cream-colored. He was as black as black could be, and she was as white as white could be. My direct boss there didn't feel comfortable doing it. I did it, and I got major flack for it, gaining a reputation as the flaming liberal minister who caused France, or at least the France in this church, to apostatize.

I felt the same rejection when, in a ministerial meeting in 1976, I had suggested that the youth could play the Carpenters at a dance at a festival there, not just the formal instrumentals that had been planned by the conservative organizers. Big mistake. For those in charge, the Carpenters were a wild rock group, and I was suggesting liberal heresy. I vowed to myself that I wouldn't speak further on this. I had accepted compromise because of my wrong identity of insecurity and rejection.

Have you ever lost hope? When I was told that I would have to go back and sell socks with my father, who had rejected and excluded me, because I was somehow "insolent" to my new boss near Lyon, I went back to my festival lodging and cried out to God for mercy, only to hear a knock on the door. I was summoned back to the ministerial meeting where I was told I would have a trial period. God rescued me there as well. The darkest night gave way to the light of day.

Our New Identity in Jesus—Restored in the Dark Time of the New Moon

For twelve years, I had been hopeless, several times coming to the brink of suicide. As the apostle Paul, I considered myself as a wretched man. At this writing, I am still endeavoring to embrace the identity I write about and that Paul finally discovered in Galatians 2:20: "I have been crucified with Christ, and it is no longer I who live, but Christ lives in me; and the life which I now live in the flesh I live by faith in [some translations say the faith *of* Christ] the Son of God, who loved me and gave himself for me."

Notice that Paul finally surrendered his old identity to Jesus, and he realized that God loved him. Have you come to know that your Father loves you?

My apostle friend who helped me see my unforgiveness used to notice my statement on my computer home page, "Robert [Bob at the time] loves Jesus." He told me it should be, "Jesus loves Robert." We begin to really love and obey God when we first know that He loves us.

Paul finally realized Jesus loved him and that the Father loved him, even though many remembered the past he remembered as well, a past of killing Christians.

Knowing in our hearts, not only in our heads, that the Father loves us, is a key to turning our hearts toward the Father in these darkest of times. Our identity must be in Jesus, who lives in us, and whom the Father loves. Paul calls Him "Christ in you, the hope of glory" (Col. 1:27).

In the darkest of times, we need to know that the Father loves us just as much as He loves Jesus. Otherwise He wouldn't have given Jesus up for us.

This truth was, I hope, bought home to me recently when a painful event occurred. Suffering rejection from one I dearly loved, I realized that person didn't care about what I was going through because it wasn't possible. The challenges were so great that a time of healing was necessary.

This situation further emphasized my identity of insecurity and rejection. I began to use a method of surrendering my pain to Jesus that all mankind will employ soon (Isa. 66:23). It's a key to returning to the Father.

The darkest time of the new moon is the time when long-term problems and burdens should be surrendered to Jesus. As the Bible says, "Sorrow may last for the night, but joy comes in the morning."

Joy begins with hope. When our identity changes from a false one that is moved by emotion at every bad circumstance, we become founded on "the hope of glory," indeed the glory Himself who lives in us.

Job speaks of the barren, desolate night in the conceptual Hebrew in chapter 3. Jesus went through a dark, dark night when He was crucified. As He rose in newness of life, we rise in Him with a new identity.

You have probably been through some dark nights. I sure have.

In one of those times recently, I laid down some of the weekly pain on the Sabbath. As I did, revelation came.

I saw Jesus on that cross, for the first time calling the Daddy He knew loved Him by the impersonal term, "God," not Father. He said, "My God, My God, why have you forsaken Me?" That was the darkest night Jesus had implored His Father to spare Him. He took all our sins and all our rejection on Himself. His Father had to turn His face away from His beloved Son for the first time ever.

The Father loved Him, yet He loved us as much, and He knew that if He didn't reject Jesus when our sin was put upon Him, the innocent Lamb of God, He couldn't have us forever.

Look At the Lamb, Not the Mirror of Your Past

In the First Testament, the offerer would present a spotless lamb for his sins. The priest wouldn't inspect the one who brought the offering. He would inspect the lamb to be sure he was spotless.

We often see ourselves as wretched, rejected people, rather than see the spotless Lamb of God who died for us and lives in us. Paul finally realized that God saw him as innocent of the blood of all men because of Jesus, no matter what he or man thought. God's opinion of Him became His identity.

As my father would often say, "That reminds me of a story."

The plane flight had been cancelled, and the wealthy businessman was impatient to rebook a flight. He rushed ahead of the line and when told by the attendant to go to the back of the line, he protested, "Do you know who I am?!"

She picked up her mike and announced on the loudspeaker: " This gentleman doesn't know who he is? Can anybody help him?"

Do we really know who we are? It may take some time for some of us to finally realize, as did Paul, how much the Father loves us, and that He and Jesus live in us. They are unshakeable and secure in us in the darkest of times. Their love never fades, even when the love of those around us and even closest to us may fade.

When our identity is in the One who loved us and gave Himself for us, we live by His hope, His faith, and His love in us. As Paul said, "But now faith, hope, love abide these three, but the greatest of these is love" (I Cor. 13:13).

The greatest love is when a man lays down his life for another, and Jesus laid down His life for all mankind. And all mankind will one day lay down their lives, surrender their insecurities, rejections, sins, and burdens to Jesus on the Sabbath and especially, for the life-long struggles, in the darkest time of the new moon.

We lay down these struggles, these false identities, on the cross. It was on that stake that the Father couldn't look on His Son because He had others He wanted in His Family with the same pedigree and status as His firstborn Son.

We sing a beautiful song at church entitled, "We Have Seen Your Glory." We had to change some of the words to fit the truth. He's not the One and only Son, but the Father's firstborn Son, since He gave up Jesus for us.

Have we seen His glory? Paul could only see his own failings for many years. He finally saw the hope of glory in him, Jesus, who became more than the hope of glory. He was the glory shining through Paul. Is He shining through us in these darkest of days?

"Jesus, we will worship You," the song continues. Worship is surrender. Jesus wanted to avoid being beaten to the unrecognizable pulp Mel Gibson couldn't possibly picture in his movie. But the only time Jesus cried out in pain was when the Father had to abandon Him. He did it, and the Father did it for us.

When we bow down on the Sabbath and in the darkest time of the new moon, we need to remember that the Father inspected the perfect Lamb of God that He loved, and He had to reject Him with our sins upon Him so we could call Him Father and Jesus Brother.

My father's nickname was Brother, but he never truly realized how much Jesus was a Brother to him or how much the Father loved him.

He was thus unable to show his son how much he loved him.

The Home Run Seen by the Father in Heaven

He was hardly ever there for me since he was a traveling salesman. He wasn't there at the height of my Little League career. I was admitted as an all-star because of my fielding, not my hitting, as we played the champion team. With two outs in the last inning, trailing by a few runs, I came to the plate, nervous as ever, with two men on base. The count became full, and the opposing coach shouted to his left fielder, "Come in. He can't hit."

As if in a dream, I swung the bat at a fastball over the plate, and hoped. The bat hit the ball and flew over the fielder's head into the bushes as I rounded third and touched home plate for a home run.

We still lost, but my joy was great, and yet Daddy wasn't there, as usual. But Daddy in heaven saw it all. The realization of His love for me is still a process. But I'm headed for a home run in that category to hear Him say, "Well done, son."

Your Father in heaven is waiting to tell you, "Well done, my son. Enter into My eternal joy." We can begin to have that joy right now, the joy of knowing in our hearts that our Father loves us as we return that love to Him and others.

A few days ago I had the privilege of speaking the words of resurrection to a dear lady in our church whose life on earth Satan had stolen. As she fell asleep and lay there in that funeral home, I spoke the right words calling her to rise. It was fully revealed afterward that she was so happy in heaven that she didn't want to be raised back into this earthly flesh.

She had heard the words, "Well done," from her Father, and had seen the glory of the firstborn of the Father. She had seen the hope of glory she had waited to see. She had seen the glory.

Have we seen His glory in us? Have we turned our hearts to the Father who loved us and loves us as much as He loves His spotless Son?

The night is darker than ever. It's time to turn our hearts to the One who loves us. For heaven's sake, let's do it. Especially for "earth's sake" let's do it, so this world will survive its darkest night ever. The fate of the earth rests with us, those the Father has drawn to Jesus now. What will we do with these truths? The world is waiting to know.

"My Father, You Forsook Jesus So You Could Have Me"

Remember what Jesus did for us. He lost the attention and concern of the Father for us. He said, "My God, My God [not My Father as He had always said], why have You forsaken Me?"

His heart was yearning to turn to the Father as He had always done, but Daddy was nowhere to be found—because of us.

For our sakes, Father Love had to turn His back, His eyes, and His ears away from His only Son at that time, His beloved Son, so He could have us in His Family, so we could turn our hearts to our Abba Father in these last days.

Our sins are covered, forgiven, and forgotten because of the blood of Jesus, His only begotten Son at that time, two thousand years ago. But now He has many Sons and Daughters. Not all have truly turned their hearts to the Father's heart in this end time where our hearts are being tested as never before.

Will we wait until the most severe shaking of believers will test us to our foundations, or will we turn our hearts now to our Father in repentance, surrender, and love—knowing how much He loves us, as much as He loves Jesus.

Jesus and the Father have bought us at a great price. The Father's heart had to turn away from His Son on that cross, so that you and I could turn our hearts to the Father before it's too late, and so that the whole earth will survive. You can be a part of that survival.

CHAPTER 24

Your Father Will Tell You How Much He Loves You!

Many are the Christians today who don't read the Bible to hear how much God loves them and who don't hear from God. If you listen to God, and He is always speaking to His sheep, He will tell you how much He loves you.

So many Christians have believed the lies of churchianity that they believe they are sinners unworthy of their Father's love. Yet if they would listen properly, they would know like John that they are the disciple whom Jesus loved.

Jesus knew the Father loved Him. His Father had told Him He was well-pleased with Him as His Son before He ever did any miraculous works. His Father's love was unconditional. Even when we sin, our Father's love and forgiveness are always available. His forgiveness is sure when we forgive, and His love is absolutely dispensed without any condition ever.

One TV evangelist admitted that He was surprised when God would thank *him* after He thanked God. He had taught that he was a rotten sinner unworthy of love, but here was God telling him how much He loved and appreciated who he was and what he was doing.

One pastor who became a charismatic pastor, speaking in tongues, had a decade of struggle to hear God's voice. He kept asking others what God's voice sounded like, and no one could tell him.

When he asked his associate pastor how to know you hear God's voice, the other pastor said, "You just know that you know." He answered, " If I knew that I knew, I wouldn't be asking you!"

Finally he spent a whole year studying how to hear from God, and God gave him the answers, principally in Habakkuk 2.

You can read the first few verses of that chapter yourself, but here is the essence of what God showed him…

Get still and be quiet before God and concentrate on Him, using whatever method you need such as soft and anointed praise and worship songs. Then just listen. You will hear spontaneous thoughts that may seem like yours but are God's, since God says you are one with Him. Then record the words as did the prophet. Write them down in two-way journaling, asking questions of God and writing His answers.

Show it to a mate or trusted friend who hears from God and knows the Bible. After a certain time you will know you are hearing from God Himself.

You may be surprised when He tells you how much He loves and appreciates you. Your heart will turn to your Father Love when you realize just how much He loves you and expresses that love to you. No words from others to the contrary will turn you from your conviction that your Father knows you and loves you with no conditions.

You will know that you know that you are hearing from God and that your Father truly loves you and will tell you what you need to do in every situation.

God's loving assurance will cast out the fears of these last days as Satan unleashes every effort to destroy true believers. Your heart will turn to your Father Love, and your prayers and life of love will cause you to save yourself and to save the earth from destruction. That's part of the message of the true gospel of the Kingdom of God. The Father is sending Jesus to save this world from utter destruction to usher in the glorious Kingdom of God on earth, and you can have a part in saving this world!

About the Author

Robert B. Scott has had forty years of experience in counselling as a pastor, shepherding churches in France, Quebec, and Edmonton, Alberta, Canada. Much revelation from the Holy Spirit and his extensive experiences enabled him by God's grace to pen God's Fruit of Forgiveness. He is the author of three other books, Why Doesn't God Heal Me?, Peace or Rejection—You Choose, and the Bible Code Broken!—The Truth about the Christian Sabbath. He has answered questions on forgiveness and family reconciliation on his Freedom Blog at both freedomchurchofgod.com and freedomtruthseekers.com. Word-of-mouth testimonies have rendered the blog virtually viral, as believers and non-believers are seeking answers to problems they have not been able to receive elsewhere.

Robert lives in Edmonton, Alberta, with his wife Lynda. He hails originally from York, South Carolina, where he accepted Jesus at the age of sixteen at a youth crusade in 1967. He remains healthy and athletic at his present age of sixty-four. He finished his high school education with honors and proceeded to receive a bachelor's degree in theology after four years of college. He began ministering as a pastor in 1972, being sent to Paris, France in 1973. In 1978 he pastored churches in Quebec City, Trois-Rivieres, and the Saguenay region of Quebec, until 1988, when he began assisting in pastoring churches in Edmonton, Alberta. In the year 2000, he and his apostolic colleague began Freedom Church of God in Edmonton, a church specializing in healing and setting God's people free. Over 600 people locally sought the healing in Jesus the church offered. Freedom Church of God acquired 1150 members in Kenya and Uganda between the years 2008 and 2011. Robert and other officials from the church and its sister foundation, Malachi 4 Foundation for Family Unity, were invited in 2010 to meet with the Minister of State in Nairobi, Kenya, to discuss the branches of the church and foundation in Kenya and their pilot fishpond project aimed at helping Kenyans to help themselves.

Robert is quite active in writing books, preparing sermons and broadcasts on their Internet radio station, and writing for the two websites. While he has not used the French he learned while preaching thousands of sermons in France and Quebec for fifteen years, he is still quite fluent in the language and is happy about contacts in French Africa and the prospect of using his skills in French to help Africans. He makes frequent voyages to Africa to serve the pastors and members there.

Printed in the United States
By Bookmasters